BAD GIRL BAKERY

To my big sister Vicky. With huge thanks for more than I can say in one sentence. I couldn't have done this without you.

First published in the UK in 2021 by
Kitchen Press Ltd
1 Windsor Place
Dundee
DD2 1BG

Text © Jeni Iannetta 2021
Photography by Clair Irwin
except: pages 2, 9, 157 & 192
by Matthias Kremer
Cover design by Kin Graphic Design
Page design by Andrew Forteath

ISBN 978-1916316553

A catalogue record for this book is available from the British Library.

Printed in India

10 9 8 7 6 5 4 3 2

BAD GIRL BAKERY

JENI IANNETTA

with

Darren Campbell, Toni Davis & Rachel Knox

Introduction

I never, ever thought I'd actually write a book. I'm a huge fan of recipe books and own far more than I'd like to admit to, so the thought of having one of our own was just plain silly. In fact, it was a running joke in the bakery; every time we came up with a new recipe we loved we'd say, 'this one will go in the book'. The truth is, even now, the team and I still can't quite believe we get to bake for a living, let alone write a book about it.

This is a book for people who love cake and love to bake. People like us, who read baking blogs or watch baking shows and get excited about the latest baking books. Whether you're a new baker or more experienced I'd like to think you'll find something you'll enjoy here.

Our baking has always been about understanding that cake is a treat. People don't tend to treat themselves as often as they used to, so when they do, it has to count. Have you ever eaten a cake and felt disappointed? That you've wasted your treat, your calories or your time baking it? At Bad Girl Bakery we want our cakes to exceed people's expectations, to be about flavour, texture, hidden surprises, generosity and impact. 'Ooft, look at that!' is something we hear a lot at our cake counter.

Our baking is not complex. We make everything by hand, just the way you do at home, and it doesn't look perfect! Douglas (Mr Bad Girl) is fond of saying that our unit of production is 'one baker, one mixer, two ovens' because we don't have any specialist machines or kit and everything we use would be at home in a domestic kitchen.

No one in our bakery team is formally trained. When I first started baking, I baked other people's recipes from books and blogs. Little by little I'd amend them and make them my own, and as time went on I took what I'd learned and began writing my own recipes. As Bad Girl grew, other people in the team brought their recipes along, and created new ones. As a result, this isn't a technical baking book; we've never really been about the process or the science. To be honest, maybe if we'd known more we might not have experimented quite so much – I'm sure technical bakers might balk at our 'let's try this and see what happens' approach.

All that said, every recipe in this book is tried and tested, they are the bakes we make and sell every day. Some are old favourites that have been on our menu since the start. Some are our take on classics or other people's bakes, or ideas and flavour combinations we like the look of. Every single recipe is shaped by our love of baking and everything we've learned from our baking heroes, tv shows, baking books and baking blogs, from courses and watching countless online tutorials and being obsessed with the latest baking trends.

We're home bakers who ended up with a bakery. You've no idea how lucky I feel and I hope you love making these recipes as much as we do.

A Bit About Bad Girl

Customers often ask about our name. It gently pokes fun at people who frown on indulgence. You know, the people who tut and say, 'Oh, you bad girl,' when you reach for a treat. (I'm pretty sure we all know someone like that.)

I got my first baking job by chance. I was a passionate home baker with no professional experience whatsoever, but Fiona Pratt, who owns Bibi's Bakery in Edinburgh, took a huge chance hiring me and I owe such a lot to her. I'm pretty sure if I hadn't met Douglas and moved to the Highlands, I'd still be at Bibi's. What I know about quality, never cutting corners and giving people a chance, I learned from Fiona.

Bad Girl was born when I moved to the Highlands. It started as a tiny, at-home bakery so I could get to know Douglas' son Felix (now absolutely my boy!).

A series of chance encounters at the right place and the right time (and, I'd like to think, good cake) meant Bad Girl grew and grew. The Highlands is a fantastic place for a business like ours with village markets, shows and food and drink fairs and we got our first big break when we were asked to fill in last minute at The Black Isle Show. Not long after, we were contacted by the Caledonian Sleeper who wanted us to supply their First Class carriages. Out of the blue, while we tried to work out how the hell we could do that operating from home, we got a call from a local farmer who'd bought up a derelict block on our village high street in Muir of Ord. It included Forbes Café, a local institution that had been closed for nearly ten years: he offered it to us and we jumped at the chance. Bad Girl Bakery Café and Cake Shop opened in 2017.

The café was a massive turning point. I still want to have a wee cry when I think about the incredible support we got, not just from the amazingly loyal customers we'd built up, but from friends and locals who offered practical help and words of encouragement. From every shelf on the walls (still holding strong, Mike), every chair that was built (thanks Colin and Gordon), to every surface cleaned (Julie, Shelia, Lizbeth, Christabel) to the walls that were painted (Dotty, you are a gem) and the huge amounts of cards and flowers from people in the village, showing their support.

The café was a massive turning point. I still want to have a wee cry when I think about the incredible support we got…

We sold out in four hours on day one and for the first few weeks there were queues around the block. Things soon snowballed, and as well as running the café and cake shop, we took over the shop unit next door to expand the wholesale side of the business, supplying local cafés (huge thanks to Velocity, Café Eighty2 and Blend), the Caledonian Sleeper and the National Trust for Scotland (what a leap of faith from Ryan Flaherty and Bart Bukowski). Another big high was supplying one of our foody heroes, Mac and Wild.

It's definitely not been plain sailing. The pandemic crushed our business, and with no tourists our wholesale business halted and the restrictions took their toll. We had to downsize, and it was heart-breaking to have to say goodbye to so many of our incredible team. But we are still here and we couldn't be more grateful. Actually grateful doesn't cover how we feel about the people that come in every week, every day sometimes. We've

gotten to know so many people over the last four years, from our lovely Sunday Morning Ladies, Jane and Winnie; to John and his daily salad; to the Thursday Morning Mums; to Roy and Anthea and the cyclists and the families that make 50-mile round trips to see us; to Anne, Alex, Sam, Sam and Amanda. We get to see the kids that come to us to have their first date, to watch young families grow up (Duncan, Alexander and Lois, we are talking about you). We see the wee ones that come in on Christmas Eve to buy a cake for Santa. We also see the space left by customers no longer with us – the lovely Mary; Mr and Mrs Storey (the sweetest couple); Morag; Mary; Ann and Graham who loved our Salted Caramel Crumble Bar.

The pandemic forced us to slow down and for the first time we had enough time on our hands to think about the business and remember why we were doing it. We spent lots of time thinking about the kind of cake we wanted to bake and for the first time really thought about our offering, where we could improve and grow. The way we baked changed dramatically. We spent lots of time researching and experimenting. What happens if we do this? What happens if we substitute this ingredient? We wrote so many new recipes that our menu post lockdown is almost unrecognisable. We are very proud of our new focus, approach and recipes: it feels like a really positive place to be and I am beyond delighted to share these recipes with you.

The Team

Our team is full of the most incredible, kind, funny, hardworking and dedicated people. Toni Davis – our head baker and my work wife – has been with us from the start.

She is the calmest person I know and makes the most incredible cookies – the Giant Chocolate Chip Cookies on page 121 are definitely her signature bake. Rachel Knox, our bakery manager, is the most meticulous, neat and precise baker I've ever met. She is the queen of Millionaire Shortbread. Darren Campbell, our head chef, makes the best burger I've ever tasted and is responsible for our savoury menu revamp. He, Toni and Rachel helped so much in the writing of this book, from their fantastic ideas to their unwavering enthusiasm and never rolling their eyes when I came up with yet another recipe for them to try.

Our general manager, Linsey Chisholm, is the most capable and organised person I've ever worked with. She does the work of two and freed me up to write this book. Julie Moran has been with us from the start and our customers love her. She comes in every day with a huge smile to cheer us all up and even manages to make Douglas laugh on his grumpiest days. Huge thanks too to Mary Fleming, who is the hardest working person I know.

And finally Mr Bad Girl, Douglas, who is fantastic at all the things I'm not (he loves a spreadsheet). He is the most incredible support and frees me up to do what I love. If it wasn't for him, there would be no Bad Girl.

There are so many special folk who are no longer working with us who deserve a mention: the lovely Lewis Mackenzie, who would have everything highly coloured and decorated if he could! Freya Turner, who made the best scones and soup, and Poppy Baker-Spink whose research on free-from baking found the recipe that inspired the cookies on page 63. There are so many others too: the ever cheery Catie Grainger and her fantastic food; Amy Storey and her amazing toasties; Christabel Chisolm and her legendary lentil soup; the lovely Fernando and his fantastic focaccia; and Sean Toye, who was an honorary member of the team for a wee while. And finally, our incredible weekend teams, who we watched grow into the most amazing young men and women. You are all missed.

What You'll Need

In my early days of baking, I was so enthusiastic I would get caught up with every baking fad and would buy all sorts of obscure specialist kit. After a couple of uses, most things ended up in the back of a drawer or at the charity shop, so you won't find many fancy gadgets here and everything we use can be found pretty easily (most from your local supermarket).

There are a few bits of equipment listed that either will make your life easier if you plan on baking a lot or are for the very few more technical recipes in the book, but they are in no way essential and are in a wee section of their own. We're definitely not suggesting you need everything on this list, but it covers everything we used when making the recipes in the book.

TINS

12-CUP MUFFIN PAN
For cupcakes and muffins. Ours are 2.5–3cm deep. The ones from the supermarket are great.

TRAYBAKE TINS
We use a 35 x 24cm tin for larger traybakes and a 32 x 21cm tin for smaller ones. Both are about 4cm deep.

23CM SPRINGFORM CAKE TIN
For single layer cakes.

20CM SANDWICH TINS
We use three of these for each of our layer cakes. We find the supermarket ones the best.

2LB LOAF TIN
We always use a 2lb loaf tin (23 x 13 x 7cm)

25CM & 23CM QUICHE/FLAN TINS
A loose bottomed tin with deep sides is best. We use a 25cm one for quiches and a 23cm one for flapjacks and tiffin (though a cake tin would do).

BAKING TRAY/COOKIE SHEET

A flat tray, the biggest you can fit in your oven, is really useful for baking biscuits and cookies.

10CM TART TINS (AT LEAST 3CM DEEP)

We use these for all our individual pies and brioche tarts.

MEASURING & WEIGHING

DIGITAL SCALES

Basic digital scales are incredibly helpful. You don't need anything fancy.

MEASURING JUG

We use a 1 litre measuring jug but it's also handy to have a small one for measuring 100ml and under.

MEASURING SPOON SET

We use these a lot! One that has tablespoon, teaspoon, half teaspoon and quarter teaspoon is ideal. We don't tend to use cup measures for anything, but they are good for measuring small amounts of liquid, so if you have them, feel free!

ICE CREAM SCOOPS

These are a godsend. We use 58mm and 47mm ones for measuring out cupcake and muffin batter – this way your cakes are all the same size and there is no mess. You definitely need ones with a scissor-action release. They are also great for icing cupcakes (see page 168).

CAKE CASES

CUPCAKES

We always use 52 x 40mm muffin cases for our cupcakes as they are a bit bigger than standard ones. You can find them in the baking section in the supermarket, labelled muffin cases.

TULIP MUFFIN WRAPS

We always use tulip muffin wraps for our muffins. Some supermarkets carry them and you'll find them online but they are very easy to make yourself and there are lots of videos online showing you how to do it. Cut baking paper into 15cm squares. Find a glass or small tin or can that fits neatly into your muffin tin hole. Place a square of baking paper over the top of the can and fold the edges, pleating them around the can to form a wrap. That's it. You can always use 52 x 40mm muffin cases instead, just reduce the baking time a little.

ICING LAYER CAKES

You can absolutely ice a layer cake with nothing but a long-handled palette knife, but if you think you might start making them regularly, here are some things to think about getting. None are expensive and they will make your life a whole lot easier.

CAKE TURNTABLE

A cake turntable makes doing your crumb coat and final layers so much easier as you can move the cake effortlessly and you run far less of a risk of putting your thumb in the icing by mistake. There are so many out there and some are super fancy, but all you need is a super simple, cheap one.

CAKE BOARDS

These are great if you're planning on gifting your cake or transporting it anywhere. The cake can be iced directly on it and any excess buttercream just wipes off. We use 10 inch, thin cake boards.

CAKE DOME

If you think you'll make a few layer cakes, it's worth investing in a cake dome that's high enough to fit over them. Then your cake can be covered when being displayed, or when leftovers are in the fridge (this might require a bit of shelf shuffling though).

MORE TECHNICAL EQUIPMENT

We're not big on fancy gadgets and unnecessary technology but there are a couple of recipes that require a bit of technical help.

KITCHEN BLOWTORCH

We use a blowtorch to finish our Meringue Frosting on cupcakes, tarts and layers and on our crème brûlée cupcakes – a small one is perfect.

DOUGH SCRAPER

A small plastic scraper is very useful for cutting and working with doughs.

JAM BAG/MUSLIN

This is a must for making the apple jelly on page 252.

A Note About Ingredients

The thing about baking is that you tend to only use a few ingredients, so each one of them has to count. We try to get as much flavour out of everything we use and the quality of the ingredients is crucial for this. Below is a list of the things we use most often: nearly everything can be bought at your local supermarket, and more specialist ingredients can easily be sourced online, but I've suggested supermarket alternatives where possible.

DARK CHOCOLATE

We always use Callebaut 70% dark chocolate. It has a lovely dark, rich flavour and colour and melts beautifully. It's easily available online but you can use any high quality 70% dark chocolate from the supermarket. Anything with a lower cocoa solid count will affect the flavour and colour of your bakes.

WHITE AND MILK CHOCOLATE

Again, we always use Callebaut white and milk chocolate, but the best quality supermarket or big brand bars work well.

EGGS

We always use medium-sized, free range eggs. We use them both for ethical reasons and because the quality is so much higher. All the recipes have been tested using medium eggs, so using other sizes will affect the outcome of your bake.

COCOA POWDER

We always use Cacao Barry Extra Brut cocoa powder, and if you're a keen baker it's really worth investing in it – you can get it easily online. Otherwise, any really good quality dark cocoa powder from the supermarket will work too; the darker the better.

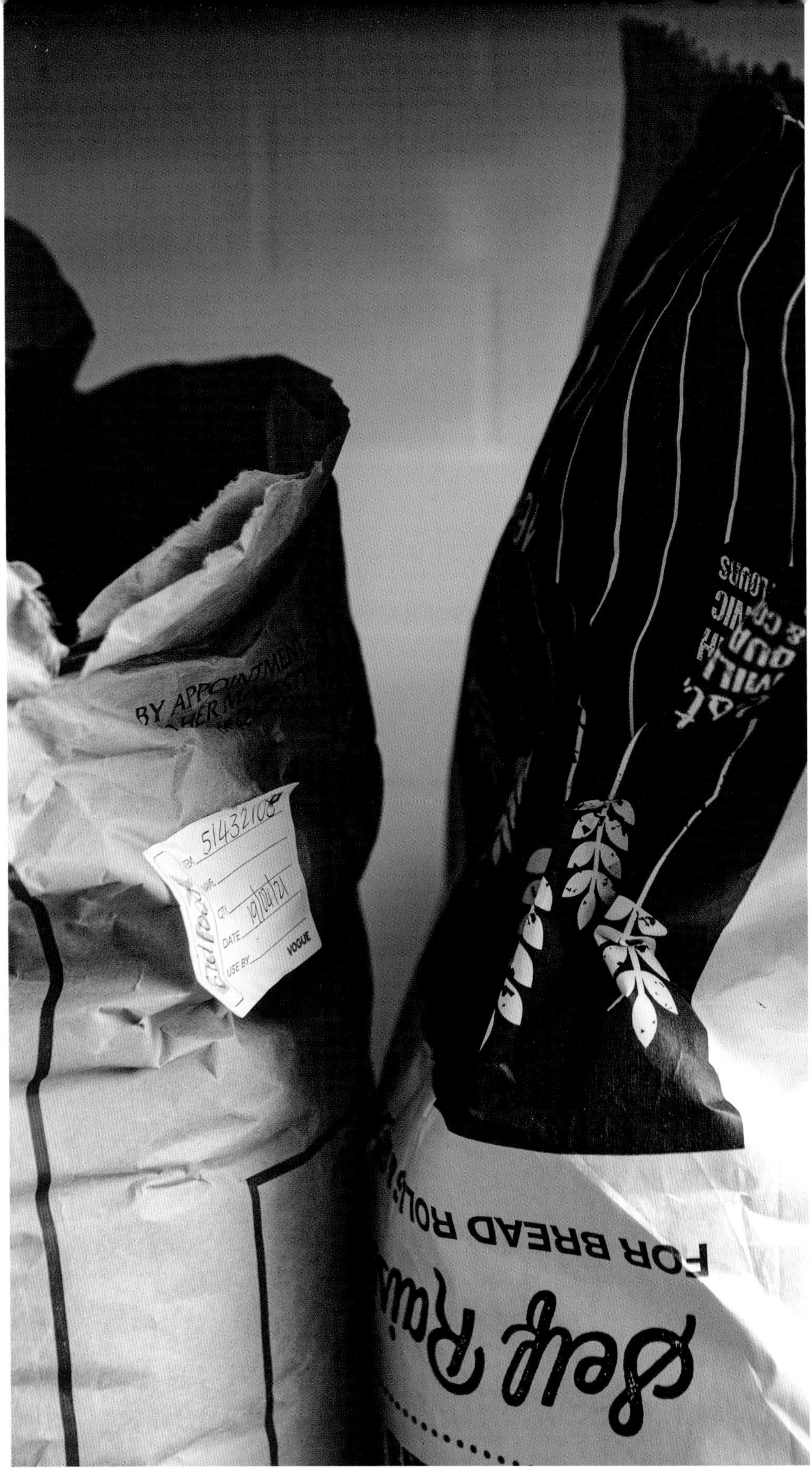
BY APPOINTMENT
USE BY
VOGUE

UNSALTED BUTTER

We always use unsalted butter, even in recipes that use salt, as that way we are in control of the salt levels. You can use baking margarine instead of butter to make the actual cakes, but (we think) they won't be as rich or as tasty. Never use marge to make buttercream though – it has to be butter.

ICING SUGAR

We buy icing sugar in bulk in big plastic bags which means it never clumps or gets lumpy. It's more likely to get lumps in it when packaged in paper, so make sure you sieve it before using.

CASTER SUGAR

We use caster rather than granulated sugar in our bakes as it is finer and dissolves quicker, and we'd recommend you do too.

VANILLA SUGAR

We make Vanilla Sugar by drying out vanilla pods after using them and leaving them in a sealed container with some caster sugar to let the flavours develop.

FLOUR

Good quality supermarket flours are great. We never sieve our flour, but if yours is a little lumpy, go ahead and give it a sieve before using.

VANILLA EXTRACT

We always use vanilla extract, not vanilla essence (which is made using artificial flavours). Extract has a stronger flavour and it's definitely worth the extra expense.

NUTS

We always toast nuts in a hot oven at 180°C (160° fan) for five to seven minutes to intensify the flavour. You can also toast them in a dry frying pan for about five minutes, moving them frequently so they don't burn.

MAPLE SYRUP

We use pure maple syrup, which is expensive, but the flavour is so strong you don't need much and we think it's definitely worth it.

Handy Hints

In this section we've included a few hints and tips you might find useful. They are by no means the only way to do things, but they work for us and might make your life easier too.

LINING TINS

ROUND CAKE TINS

We grease both the sides and bottoms of our tins, but we only ever line the bottom. Cut a circle of greaseproof to the same size as the base, using the tin as a template. If your tin is a little older and less non-stick, you might want to line the sides too. If so, line the bottom and then cut separate strips of paper 2–3cm higher than the sides of the tin. Using the greased sides, stick the paper strips flat against the sides, making sure there are no wrinkles, or they will show on the cake.

LOAF TIN

We don't grease our loaf tins. Cut two strips of paper; one strip cut exactly to fit the base of the tin lengthwise and one cut exactly to fit width-wise. Make sure the strips are long enough to hang over the sides; that way you can use them to lift the baked cake out. The flaps of paper can also be folded over the cake mid-bake if it's browning too much.

QUICHE/FLAN TIN

We don't grease these either. The easiest thing to do is to cut a piece of paper larger than the diameter of the tin, then crumple it up to make the paper soft and supple, then smooth it into the tin.

I saw Jamie Oliver do this years ago and we've done it ever since!

TRAYBAKE TIN

Again, we don't grease traybake tins. Just cut a sheet of greaseproof paper larger than the tin and push it into place, pleating the corners so it sits in them neatly. If the paper is in one piece you can use it to lift the whole traybake out of its tin.

BAKING TRAY

We always line our baking trays, and because our oven fans are so powerful, we put some oven-proof cutlery on the edges of the paper to hold it down.

BAKING TIMES

All ovens are different, so always test cakes to see if they're done. We do like big generous bakes, but if you would like to make your biscuits or muffins a little smaller, just reduce the baking time accordingly.

HOW TO TEST TO SEE IF CAKES ARE DONE

We always use metal BBQ skewers to test our cakes, but any cake tester or skewer will do. Always test the thickest part and/or the centre of each cake. When the skewer comes out clean and dry, your cake is ready. With sponges, if the top is firm and springy, that's a good sign too. When making cupcakes, muffins and layers, test each one in the batch as they may bake at different rates depending on size and where they are in the oven.

MELTING CHOCOLATE

We always melt chocolate over a pan of just-simmering water. Keep the heat low and make sure the water doesn't touch the bottom of the bowl or get anywhere near the chocolate. We take the chocolate off the heat when it's almost melted, with a few bits just holding their shape. The heat in the bowl will finish it off and you won't run the risk of overheating it.

You can melt chocolate in a microwave on medium in short 20-second bursts, giving it a little stir between each, but you do run the risk of burning it. Burnt chocolate smells terrible!

FILLING PIPING BAGS

It's always easier to do this if you use a large piping bag. Pop your nozzle in and then, holding the bag in one hand, turn the top third down over your hand. Spoon the buttercream in, closing your fingers over the spatula through the bag to scrape the buttercream off. Fill the bag until it's two thirds full (and no more), working the buttercream down the bag towards the nozzle, then turn the top of the bag back up.

BLIND BAKING

Line your tins with pastry, pricking the base with a fork, then cover with a scrunched up piece of greaseproof slightly bigger than the tin. Fill with baking beans, uncooked lentils or rice to weigh the paper down.

CUTTING CAKES

LAYER CAKES, SINGLE LAYER CAKES AND LOAVES

We use a long, non-serrated knife and gently push it down without sawing backwards and forwards. If the cake is iced with buttercream, it will cut better if the buttercream is a little firm – if it's not, pop it in the fridge for five minutes or so.

TRAYBAKES

For anything covered in chocolate (like millionaire and tiffin), fill a tall jug with hot water and put the blade of your knife in to heat up. A non-serrated, deep knife works best. Dry the blade off, then press the length of the hot knife into the chocolate, pushing gently. You'll see the chocolate melt a little and the knife will slide through it, then cut through whatever is underneath. Heat and dry the knife before every cut.

STORING CAKES

Our cakes are best eaten on the day, but some may keep for up to two to three days if stored cool and covered. Muffins, scones and brioche are only ever good on the day. Bakes decorated with buttercream or fresh fruit are really best eaten on the day they are made, but leftovers can be stored in the fridge and eaten the next day.

Cake
Break

The moment we started talking about this book, I knew I really wanted to have a section called Cake for Breakfast. The lovely Amy North, editor of *British Baker*, interviewed me for a piece about sticky buns and I remember telling her that I thought sticky buns, cinnamon buns and brioche were all perfectly acceptable to eat in the morning. She says she thinks about that every time she wants to justify something indulgent for breakfast!

If you want an occasional treat that can be enjoyed in the morning, this is where you'll find it. While you probably don't want a big slab of chocolate cake or an iced cupcake first thing (but no judgement here if you do), you might fancy a muffin, scone or breakfast pastry.

We used to be very wary of any recipes that involved yeast, and it was only through lots of research and (most importantly) getting help and advice from Graeme Ayton at Scottish Bakers that we got to grips with brioche. Turns out it's actually not that scary, especially if you have a stand mixer, and now we use brioche dough as a base recipe for some of our favourite breakfast bakes.

The recipes in this chapter vary from really simple, one-bowl muffin recipes to more time-consuming (but not difficult) recipes like the brioche tarts and Cardamom & White Chocolate Sticky Buns. The flavours are inspired by breakfast: the Breakfast Smoothie Muffin is made with a breakfast smoothie, oats feature a lot and the Granola, Greek Yoghurt & Berry Muffins are made with breakfast granola. However understated some of the bakes in this chapter may sound, they are still generous and indulgent, and all of them are treats.

We hope you enjoy them.

For fast

Granola, Greek Yoghurt & Berry Muffins GF

These muffins are a favourite on our breakfast menu. They can be made quickly in the morning and are absolutely delicious served warm with a dollop of Greek yoghurt and some berries or Berry Compote (page 251) on the side. If you're not gluten free, you can make them with standard granola, flour and baking powder – just leave out the xanthan gum.

- Leftovers can be split and toasted in a hot pan and served with butter, jam or fruit compote.

- Don't leave out the xanthan gum or the muffins will be very crumbly.

MAKES 6 LARGE MUFFINS

6-cup muffin tin
6 large tulip muffin wraps
  (page 9)

75g gluten-free self-raising flour
125g desiccated coconut
2 tsp gluten-free baking powder
½ tsp xanthan gum
100g full-fat Greek yoghurt
2 medium eggs
1 tsp vanilla extract
150g unsalted butter, softened
150g soft light brown sugar
65g gluten-free granola
75g raspberries or blueberries
salt

To finish (optional):
12–15 extra berries
50g gluten-free granola
20g coconut flakes or desiccated
  coconut

Preheat the oven to 190°C (170°C fan). Weigh the flour, coconut, baking powder and xanthan gum into a bowl with a pinch of salt and give them a quick mix to combine. Weigh the yoghurt into a jug, then add the eggs and vanilla and give it a stir.

Cream the butter and sugar together in a large bowl until soft and light in colour. Pour in the yoghurt and eggs and mix, then stir in the flour and coconut mix until the dry ingredients are nearly combined. You want to be able to see some dry flour in the mix. Add in the granola and berries and give it a final, gentle stir. Again, you want the batter to be only just combined.

Divide the batter between the six wraps and press a few berries over the top of each one. Sprinkle over the remaining granola and coconut flakes if using.

Bake on the middle shelf of your oven for 30 to 35 minutes, but check with a skewer after 25. The muffins are ready when the skewer comes out clean and dry and the tops feel springy to the touch.

Leave to cool in the tin for ten minutes, then serve warm, or transfer to a wire rack to cool completely if you want to eat them later.

Chocolate Chip Pancake Muffins

To us these taste like pancakes, and the name has stuck. They are the perfect weekend breakfast treat, served warm from the oven with a strong cup of coffee. They take no time to make and all you need is a bowl and a spatula – you can weigh out all the dry ingredients the night before, making it even easier to whip up a batch in the morning. Any leftovers are delicious toasted the next day (see page 263).

· This is a really simple wet-into-dry recipe and the only thing to remember is that the trick to light muffins is not to overmix them.

MAKES 8 LARGE MUFFINS

12-cup muffin pan
8 large tulip muffin wraps
   (page 9)

300g self-raising flour
150g soft light brown sugar
50g caster sugar
300ml evaporated milk
150g unsalted butter, melted
3 medium eggs
2 tsp vanilla extract
200g milk chocolate chips
   (or a bar, chopped into
   small chunks)
salt

To finish:
50g milk chocolate chips
   (optional)

Heat the oven to 200°C (180°C fan).

Pop the muffin wraps in the muffin pan. Weigh out the flour and the light brown and caster sugars into a big bowl with a pinch of salt and mix to combine. If there are lumps of brown sugar, just rub them in with your fingers, as if you were making crumble.

Measure the evaporated milk into a jug and add the melted butter, eggs and vanilla. Give it a whisk to combine – make sure it's well mixed as the less mixing you have to do later, the better!

Pour the eggy milk over the dry ingredients and mix gently until nearly combined. You want to be able to see some dry flour in the mix. Add the chocolate chips and give a final gentle stir. Again, you want the mix to be only just combined.

Divide the batter equally between the muffin wraps with a large ice cream scoop if you have one (or a spoon if you don't), scraping the bowl down to get every last drop. The wraps will look very full. Dot the tops with the extra chocolate chips if you're using them.

cont.

Preheat the oven to 200°C (180°C fan). Push the centre of the risen dough base down a little to make space for the filling, then place two tablespoons of caramel in the centre of each one, followed by a few banana slices and then some pecans.

Glaze any exposed dough with the beaten egg and bake on the top shelf of the oven for 15 to 20 minutes, or until the dough is dark golden brown and a skewer comes out clean when inserted into the rim of the tart. Allow to cool for ten minutes before removing from the tin.

Drizzle the tarts with leftover caramel and serve while still warm.

HAND METHOD

Knead the dough by hand until it is smooth and stretchy – it will take a bit of time. Use cubes of very soft butter and add them a few at a time to the dough, kneading until completely incorporated. The dough will break and look craggy and the process is very messy, but persevere and it will come together. You'll need a dough scraper to scrape the excess butter off your counter and back into your dough.

Berries & Custard Brioche Traybake

This is a really easy brioche recipe, and it's so pretty to look at. It makes a lovely birthday breakfast and is a great option if you're feeding a crowd.

- The dough needs to be refrigerated overnight so get started the day before you want to eat it.

- If you don't have time to make your own, you can use good quality, bought custard instead – the fresh kind you find in the fridge at the supermarket is best.

SERVES 8–10

32 x 21cm traybake tin, lightly greased with vegetable oil

For the dough:
200g strong white bread flour
50g plain flour
40g caster sugar (we use Vanilla Sugar, page 17)
1 tsp salt
7g sachet fast action yeast
60ml milk (slightly warmed)
3 medium eggs
125g unsalted butter, cubed and softened

For the filling:
1 batch of Custard Filling (page 255), cooled
125g raspberries
125g blueberries

To finish:
1 egg for glazing, beaten

Weigh out the strong and plain flour, sugar and salt into the bowl of your stand mixer and give them a stir to mix. Add the yeast, milk and eggs and mix on low for two to three minutes, then increase to medium for 10 to 15 minutes. Scrape down the bowl and paddle a couple of times during mixing.

By now your dough should be smooth-looking and stretchy (give it a wee pull to check). With the mixer still on low, add two to three cubes of butter at a time. You can't rush this stage, I'm afraid, so don't add any more butter until you can't see any trace of the last lot.

Keep adding the butter two to three cubes at a time until it's all gone, and keep mixing until the dough has come away from the sides of the mixer. Scrape the dough out and put it in a well-oiled bowl, then cover with lightly oiled cling film and pop in the fridge overnight.

Next morning, give the dough a punch to knock the air out and press the dough into an even layer in the bottom of your greased tin. Cover with cling film and put it somewhere warm until the dough doubles in size.

cont.

Make the Custard Filling on page 255 and allow it to cool a little before popping in the fridge to cool completely.

Preheat the oven to 200°C (180°C fan). Leaving a border of 2–3cm around the edge, push the dough down a little to create space for the filling. Spoon in the custard, then scatter over the raspberries and blueberries.

Glaze any exposed dough with beaten egg and bake on the top shelf of the oven for 25 minutes, or until the dough is golden brown and a skewer inserted into the edge comes out clean. Allow to cool for ten minutes before you tear into it.

Serve while still warm.

HAND METHOD

Knead the dough by hand until it is smooth and stretchy – it will take a bit of time. Use cubes of very soft butter and add them a few at a time to the dough, kneading until completely incorporated. The dough will break and look craggy and the process is very messy, but persevere and it will come together. You'll need a dough scraper to scrape the excess butter off your counter and back into your dough.

Cardamon & White Chocolate Sticky Buns

Sticky buns are a big hit in the bakery, and we often have customers queuing for them in the mornings. These sticky buns are soft and squidgy, perfect for a special breakfast or Sunday brunch. They are lightly spiced, sweet with white chocolate and finished with a vanilla milk glaze. If you've never made yeasted dough before, this is a simple place to start; the beauty of the recipe is that everything is done the day before.

- The buns need to be refrigerated overnight, so get started the day before you want to eat them.

- Don't add a lot of flour when rolling out the dough as it can dry it out.

- When you're rolling up the dough, lift the dough as you roll it up so you don't push out the filling as you go.

- These are only good on the day they are made, but you can make Sticky Bun French Toast (page 265) with any leftovers.

MAKES 8 LARGE BUNS

35 x 24cm traybake tin, lined

For the dough:
500g strong white bread flour
75g caster sugar
1 tsp ground cardamom
75g unsalted butter, cubed
1 tsp sea salt
2 x 7g sachets fast action yeast
275ml whole milk
2 medium eggs, beaten

Put the flour, sugar and cardamom in a large bowl, then rub in the butter until it looks like breadcrumbs. Add the salt on one side of the bowl, the yeast on the other and make a well in the middle. Pour in the milk and the beaten eggs and stir with a butter knife until you have a rough ball of sticky dough. You can do this in a stand mixer if you like.

Sprinkle a little flour on the work surface and knead the dough until it is soft and smooth and can stretch easily. This will take about 15 to 20 minutes by hand, or half that time if using a mixer.

Place the dough in an oiled bowl, cover with cling film and leave somewhere warm until it doubles in size. How long it takes to rise will vary depending on how warm your kitchen is.

cont.

For the filling:
100g caster sugar
50g light brown sugar
2 tsp ground cardamom
100g unsalted butter, very soft
150g white chocolate chips
    or chunks

For the glaze:
300g icing sugar
4–5 tbsp milk
1 tsp vanilla extract

While that's rising, make your filling. Mix the caster and light brown sugars with the cardamom. Once the dough has risen, give it a punch to knock the air out (very satisfying!), then roll it on a lightly floured counter into a rectangle about 50 x 25cm with the long edge closest to you.

Spread the soft butter over the dough using your fingers, then scatter over the sugar mixture followed by a layer of white chocolate chips. Starting from the long edge in front of you, roll the dough up tightly so you end up with a long, fat sausage and use your hands to even it out. Cut off the ragged ends, then slice into eight even pieces. For each one, take the very edge of the dough and pull it under the bun (see pic) to stop all the filling running out. Place the buns in your lined tin so they have room to rise and ease open the layers a little. Cover with cling film and place in the fridge overnight.

Next morning, take out of the fridge and put in a warm place until the buns double in size and fill the tray. Preheat the oven to 200°C (180°C fan). Bake for 25 to 30 minutes until the buns are dark and a skewer comes out clean. Let them sit for 10 minutes while you whisk the icing sugar, milk and vanilla together to form a thick glaze, then drizzle it over the buns just before you serve them.

Variations

CARAMEL PECAN CINNAMON
Replace the cardamon with ground cinnamon and fill with chopped pecans instead of white chocolate. Drizzle with caramel after baking.

SAVOURY SWIRLS
Omit the cardamon in the dough and fill with five or six tablespoons of pesto (enough for a thin layer across the dough) and 100g grated mozzarella. To serve, scatter over some sea salt flakes, basil leaves and a drizzle of olive oil.

Raspberry Doughnut Brioche Buns

These buns are a cross between a muffin and a doughnut and make a lovely special-occasion breakfast. The recipe makes six buns, but if you double it you'll have leftovers to make the Brioche Bread & Butter Pudding on page 266.

- The dough needs to be refrigerated overnight so get started the day before you want to eat them.

- These are best eaten on the day they're made.

MAKES 6 BUNS

6-cup muffin tin
6 large tulip muffin wraps
   (page 9)

For the dough:
200g strong white bread flour
50g plain flour
40g caster sugar (we use
   Vanilla Sugar, see page 17)
1 tsp ground cinnamon
½ tsp salt
3 medium eggs
60ml milk, slightly warmed
7g sachet fast action yeast
125g unsalted butter,
   cubed and softened
vegetable oil for greasing

To finish:
1 egg for glazing, beaten
20g unsalted butter, melted
2 tbsp caster sugar
¼ tsp ground cinnamon
½ jar raspberry jam

Weigh out the strong and plain flours, sugar, cinnamon and salt into the bowl of your stand mixer and give them a stir to mix. Add the eggs, milk and yeast and mix on low speed for two to three minutes, then increase to medium for 10 to 15 minutes. Scrape down the bowl and paddle a couple of times during mixing.

By now your dough should be smooth-looking and stretchy (give it a wee pull to check). With the mixer still on low, add two or three cubes of butter at a time. You can't rush this stage, I'm afraid, so don't add any more butter until you can't see any trace of the last lot.

Keep adding the butter two to three cubes at a time until it's all gone, and keep mixing until the dough has come away from the sides of the mixer. Scrape the dough out and put it in a well-oiled bowl, then cover with cling film and pop in the fridge overnight.

Next morning, give the dough a punch to knock the air out. Divide into six and roll each piece into a smooth ball. Put the muffin wraps into the tin, then put a ball of dough in each one and cover with cling film. Put somewhere warm until the balls double in size.

cont.

Preheat the oven to 200°C (180°C fan). Glaze each dough ball with the beaten egg and bake on the top shelf of the oven for 15 to 20 minutes, until they're golden brown and a skewer inserted into the middle comes out clean. Leave to cool in the tin for ten minutes.

When they're cool enough to handle, use an apple corer or a small sharp knife to core out the centre of each bun and paint the tops with melted butter. Combine the remaining caster sugar and cinnamon, then sprinkle it over the buns, making sure some goes down the hole. Fill with the raspberry jam and serve while still warm.

HAND METHOD
Knead the dough by hand until it is smooth and stretchy – it will take a bit of time. Use cubes of very soft butter and add them two or three at a time to the dough, kneading until completely incorporated. The dough will break and look craggy, and the process is very messy, but persevere and it will come together. You'll need a dough scraper to scrape the excess butter off your counter and back into your dough.

Variations

LEMON DRIZZLE BRIOCHE BUNS
Replace the cinnamon in the dough with lemon zest. Fill with lemon curd and top with a thick drizzle made with lemon juice and caster sugar.

Breakfast Pastries

These beautiful breakfast pastries are perfect for a birthday breakfast or weekend brunch. We've included a few of our favourite fillings here but the possibilities are endless and you can make lots of different flavours in one batch, using up fruit, berries and jam. To make vegan pastries, use the same quantity of home-made Vegan Rough Puff Pastry or ready-rolled shop-bought vegan pastry, and use plant-based milk to glaze.

MAKES 4 PASTRIES

large baking tray, lined

½ batch of Rough Puff Pastry
    or Vegan Rough Puff Pastry
    (pages 277-280) or 1 x 375g
    ready-rolled puff pastry
1 batch of filling
1 egg beaten with a splash of milk
icing sugar for dusting

Preheat the oven to 200°C (180°C fan).

Lightly flour your work surface and roll out your pastry into a square about 30 x 30cm. Don't worry if your edges are raggedy; they will be trimmed off. If you're using shop-bought pastry, you may need to roll it out a little more than it already is.

Trim the pastry to a 25cm square, then cut it into quarters to give you four 12.5cm squares.

Spread the caramel, curd, custard, jam or apple jelly diagonally across the centre of each square and arrange the fruit on top. Don't spread the filling to the edges of the pastry – there should be about 2cm of bare pastry at either corner (so the filling won't ooze out of the pastry on baking).

Dab a little egg wash (or plant-based milk) on one of the corners opposite the long edge of the filling, then fold the opposite corner into the middle of the square. Fold the egg washed corner on top (the egg wash/milk is the glue that holds the pastry together) and press the join down with a fork.

Egg wash the tops of the pastries or glaze with plant-based milk, place on your lined baking tray and sprinkle over the nuts if using. Bake on the middle shelf for 20 to 25 minutes, or until the pastry is golden brown.

Allow to sit on the baking tray for five minutes before dusting with icing sugar and serving. They don't really keep so eat them the day you make them.

cont.

Fillings:

APPLE, CARAMEL & HAZELNUT
3 generous tbsp caramel

2 large apples, peeled, cored and each
cut into 8 thick slices, then cooked in
1 tbsp of butter and 1 tbsp of brown sugar
until they begin to soften

4 tbsp skinned and blanched hazelnuts,
roughly chopped

BLUEBERRY & LIME
3 generous tbsp lime curd

about 100g blueberries (we use around
10 per pastry)

BANANA & CUSTARD
3 generous tbsp custard filling

2 large bananas cut into thick slices and
sprinkled with soft brown sugar once
they are placed on the pastry

LEMON, RASPBERRY & ALMOND
3 generous tbsp lemon curd

16 raspberries (4 per pastry)

4 tbsp flaked almonds

APPLE & ALMOND (V)
4 generous tbsp apple jelly

2 large apples peeled, cored and each
cut into 8 thick slices, then cooked in
1 tbsp of plant-based spread and 1 tbsp
of brown sugar until they begin to soften

4 tbsp flaked almonds

PB&J (V)
3 generous tsp raspberry jam

3 tsp nut butter

16 raspberries (4 per pastry)

APRICOT & PISTACHIO (V)
3 generous tbsp apricot jam

410g tin peach slices
(we use 3 or 4 per pastry)

4 tsp pistachios, roughly chopped

Dark Chocolate, Cranberry & Coconut Flapjack

GF

This flapjack is the kind of thing you'd bake for someone who says they don't really like cake. There's something about the combination of oats and dried fruit that makes it seem like it's a healthier choice: it's practically cereal! The thing that makes this flapjack, we think, is that it's soft, very, very buttery and not at all dry. It's a great recipe to have up your sleeve because you can add to it any dried fruit or nuts you fancy and come up with a different flavour every time.

MAKES 8 GENEROUS WEDGES

25cm round flan or cake tin or
    31 x 21cm traybake tin, bottom
    and sides lined with one large
    piece of baking paper

400g gluten-free porridge oats
    (not jumbo or oatmeal)
200g dried cranberries
50g desiccated coconut
150g 70% dark chocolate,
    chips or chopped
250g unsalted butter, cubed
150g light brown sugar
5 tbsp honey
5 tbsp golden syrup

To finish:
200g 70% dark chocolate, melted
20g dried cranberries
10g desiccated coconut

Preheat the oven to 180°C (160°C fan). Weigh the oats, cranberries and coconut into a bowl big enough to hold all the ingredients. Weigh the chocolate chips into a separate bowl.

Weigh the butter, sugar, honey and syrup straight into a saucepan and put over a low heat until the butter has melted, then set aside to cool for a few minutes. You don't want the mixture to be hot enough to melt the chocolate.

Pour the cooled butter mix into the oats and stir until everything is well covered. Press half of the mixture into the bottom of the tin and then scatter over the chocolate chips. Top with the rest of the mixture and press it down flat.

Bake on the middle shelf for about 25 minutes or until the edges are just golden brown – it will look very soft but hold your nerve! Leave to cool and firm up in the tin.

The trickiest part about this recipe is waiting for it to cool so you can cut and decorate the flapjacks. Trust us, it will fall apart if you try to pick up a warm piece.

cont.

Cranberry, Clementine & White Chocolate Scones

These scones are a real favourite at Christmas time, when we always make them with fresh cranberries. They're just as good with dried cranberries, and you can use the zest of a large orange instead of the two clementines if you fancy. Just like the savoury scones, you can change up the flavours really easily by replacing the cranberries, zest and chocolate with different combinations of sweet flavours. We've given you a few of our favourite combinations to try on page 57.

- The best tip we can give is don't overwork the dough. Overworked dough makes your scones heavy – it should have lumps and bumps in it.

- The consistency of the dough is the only tricky thing here. After making this a few times you'll know exactly what you're looking for. Too dry and your scones will be dense and crumbly; too wet and sticky, they won't rise and will be tough and chewy.

- Scones are at their very best served still warm from the oven and are definitely only good on the day. They can be frozen though: once defrosted, refresh them in the oven for a wee while to warm through. Don't decorate the top of scones you are planning to freeze.

cont.

Every
Treats

Everyday Treats to us are bakes that are either super simple to make, or a little (but only a little) less indulgent than the cakes in other chapters.

Some are bakes you could tackle midweek without too much stress, like the Caramel Brownie, the Coconut, Chilli & Lime Cake or the Double Chocolate Muffin: all one-bowl recipes that just need a bit of light stirring. Some are everyday sort of bakes given a Bad Girl twist, like the Milk Chocolate 'Digestive' Biscuits, Giant Lemon Drizzles or Pimped-up Shortbread. Others – like the tiffin, Salted Caramel Crumble Bar or Raspberry & White Chocolate Cookie Bars – are perfect for a bake sale, work celebration or feeding a crowd. The loaves – both the Cranberry, Almond and Yoghurt and the Blueberry, Coconut and Lime – I've tagged as 'everyday' because they are plain, undecorated and simple to look at. Don't be fooled by their appearance though; they are packed with flavour and are most definitely indulgent.

What all the recipes have in common is they are super simple to make. There are no complicated processes – there might be a couple of steps in some of the recipes, but none are difficult.

Don't let this chapter heading fool you though. 'Everyday' definitely doesn't mean dull! These bakes may be slightly less indulgent than some of our others, but they are most definitely treats.

day

Using a small ice cream scoop or a soup spoon, place 12 golf ball-sized blobs of dough onto the baking sheets, giving them plenty of space to spread. (You may only get four to five on each sheet.) Pop the trays in the oven for 17 minutes but check them after 15. When the cookies are ready they'll still look soft but not wet. If they don't look ready, give them another two minutes. Leave to cool completely before lifting them off the trays. If you try to move them when they're warm they are more likely to stick to the paper and break. If you find they are still sticking a little even when cool, run a palette knife under them to loosen them.

Variations

CHOCOLATE ORANGE COOKIES
Add the zest of an orange with the dry ingredients.

GIANT ICE CREAM SANDWICH
We serve two of these cookies sandwiched together with ice cream on our street food menu – they always go down a storm.

Milk Chocolate 'Digestive' Biscuits

As home bakers with no formal training, most of our recipes are as a result of trying a bit of this and a bit of that. I came across a book called *Ratio* by Michael Ruhlman in which he says, 'When you know a culinary ratio, it's not like knowing a single recipe, it's like instantly knowing a thousand.' His ratio for a basic cookie dough is one part sugar: two parts fat: three parts flour. I loved the idea, so we set about trying it out and our take on digestive biscuits was born. These are so simple to make, especially in a food processor.

· If you prefer an oaty biscuit, replace 50g of the flour with 50g porridge oats (not jumbo oats or oatmeal).

· If you want a more classic digestive look, you can cover the top of the biscuits with the melted chocolate using a spatula instead of dipping them.

MAKES 8 THICK, GENEROUS BISCUITS

2 large baking sheets, lined
9cm scone or cookie cutter

100g caster sugar (we use vanilla
    caster sugar, see page 17)
200g unsalted butter, straight from
    the fridge, cut into small cubes
300g plain wholemeal flour
    (plus a little extra for dusting)
1 tsp baking powder
3–4 tsp milk
salt

To finish:
200g milk chocolate

Preheat the oven to 180°C (160°C fan).

If you're using a food processor, all you need to do is whizz together the sugar, butter, flour, baking powder and a pinch of salt until the mixture looks like breadcrumbs and there are no big lumps of butter. Tip the mix into a big bowl. If you're doing it by hand, just rub in the butter with your fingertips – it will take a bit longer. Give the bowl a shake and any rogue lumps of butter will come to the top – rub them in too.

When you have your breadcrumb-like mix in your bowl, add three teaspoons of milk and work it in using your fingers until everything starts coming together to form a crumbly dough. If you need to, add another teaspoon of milk. Form the dough into a ball: it will look crumbly and you might think there's no way it will come together, but it will. Dust your work surface with a little flour and flatten your ball of dough into a disc. Roll it out to the thickness of about a centimetre, moving the dough around a little on your work surface to stop it sticking.

cont.

Cut out eight biscuits – you might need to re-roll the dough a couple of times. Space them out on the lined baking trays and prick each biscuit all over with a fork.

Bake for 20 to 25 minutes, until the biscuits are a dark golden brown (a little more so round the edges). They won't be firm to the touch, but they will harden as they cool. Leave to cool completely on the trays. To finish, melt the chocolate in a small, deep, heatproof bowl either in the microwave or over just-simmering water. Dip half of each biscuit in the melted chocolate and pop them back on the baking trays to set.

Caramelised White Chocolate & Pecan Shortbread

It's really worth making the extra effort to caramelise some white chocolate for these shortbread biscuits. It takes a little time and patience, but we think it's worth it for the nutty, caramelly flavour. The recipe is on page 249 – we usually caramelise the chocolate the day before we're baking as it needs to cool and harden before using. Feel free to make the shortbread with un-caramelised white chocolate. It will taste lovely too!

MAKES 8 GENEROUS BISCUITS

2 baking sheets, lined
9cm scone or cookie cutter

For the shortbread:
250g plain flour
 (plus more for dusting)
75g cornflour
115g soft dark brown sugar
250g unsalted butter,
 chopped into small cubes
100g pecans, roasted and
 chopped
100g Caramelised White
 Chocolate, chopped into
 chunks (page 249)

To finish:
200g Caramelised White
 Chocolate, melted
100g pecans, roasted
 and chopped

Preheat the oven to 180°C (160°C fan).

Weigh the plain flour, cornflour and sugar into your bowl and give it a little mix to combine. Add the butter and, picking up little handfuls of the mix, rub the butter in between your thumb and fingers (as though you're making crumble) until it looks like breadcrumbs. Stir in the pecans and the Caramelised White Chocolate chunks until the dough starts to come together and it looks more like rubble. If you're using a mixer, do the same steps on a low speed.

Bring the dough together into a ball with your hands and put it on a lightly floured surface.

Flatten it into a fat disc and sprinkle a tiny bit of flour over the top, then roll it out to about a centimetre thick – don't be tempted to roll the biscuits thinner or the nuts are likely to poke out of the dough and burn as they bake. Keep moving the dough a little as you roll it, rotating it so it doesn't stick.

Swirl your cutter in the flour on your work surface then cut out eight rounds, re-rolling the dough a couple of times.

cont.

Because this recipe (very satisfyingly!) uses all the dough with no leftovers, we make the last biscuit by putting the last of the dough inside the cutter and flattening it out with our fingers. If you have finger marks on the biscuit, just turn it over so the uneven side is on the baking sheet.

Pop the cut-out biscuits on the lined baking sheets with a little space between them. Pop the baking sheets in the fridge to chill for 20 minutes or in the freezer for ten minutes.

Bake the chilled biscuits for 25 to 30 minutes. Really the only way to tell these are done is by colour, though do bear in mind that they use dark brown sugar so they bake to a darker colour than traditional shortbread. When they are ready, they will be deep golden brown, a bit like the colour of a digestive biscuit. The colour may be a bit deeper round the edges and the middles will be almost firm. They will harden more as they cool.

Leave the biscuits to cool completely on the trays while you melt the remaining Caramelised White Chocolate, either in bursts in a microwave on low or in a small, deep heatproof bowl over some just-simmering water.

When the biscuits are cool, dip half of each one in the melted chocolate, put back on the baking sheet and scatter over the pecans before the chocolate sets.

Either pop them in the fridge or leave in a cool place for a little while until the chocolate hardens.

Variations

HAZELNUT, CARDAMOM & MILK CHOCOLATE SHORTBREAD

Bake as per the recipe but use 115g soft light brown sugar instead of dark, and add 1½ tsp ground cardamom to the flour mix when you're making the dough. Replace the pecans in the dough with the same quantity of chopped roasted hazelnuts. Finish by dipping the biscuits in 150g melted milk chocolate and scattering with 50g chopped roasted hazelnuts.

CRANBERRY, ORANGE & WHITE CHOCOLATE SHORTBREAD

Bake as per the recipe but use 115g caster sugar instead of brown, and replace the pecans in the dough with 100g dried cranberries and the zest of an orange. When the biscuits are cool, dip them in 150g melted white chocolate and scatter with another 50g dried cranberries before the chocolate sets. These won't bake as dark as the other variations, so bake until the tops feel almost firm to the touch and the edges are the lightest shade of golden brown.

TRIPLE CHOCOLATE SHORTBREAD

Bake as per the recipe but use 115g soft light brown sugar instead of dark, and replace the pecans in the dough with 125g chocolate chips (we use a mix of white and milk). When the biscuits are cool, dip them in 150g melted dark chocolate.

Caramel Brownie

This is the basic brownie recipe we use in the shop. It's a mixture between cakey and fudgey so creates the perfect base for gooey pockets of caramel in every portion. There's a more indulgent brownie in the next chapter, but this one is more of an everyday bake: quick to put together in a hurry and lovely served warm as a pudding.

- You can use gluten-free flour (we use Doves Farm self-raising). The texture will be slightly different but still lovely.

- When you're baking brownies, never go by time alone: every oven is different so always do a skewer test. I'm not a fan of under-baked brownies; slightly fudgey is great but raw is not good at all!

- This brownie is at its absolute best on the day it's baked and is still really good the day after, though on day two you might want to warm it though in the microwave and have it with some cream or ice cream.

MAKES 12

35 x 24cm traybake tin, lined

350g good 70% dark chocolate, chips or chopped
300g unsalted butter, cubed
200g caster sugar
200g light brown sugar
6 medium eggs
2 tsp vanilla extract
75g plain flour
75g self-raising flour
300g shop-bought caramel or ½ batch of Soft Caramel (page 244)
salt

Preheat the oven to 180°C (160°C fan).

Weigh your chocolate and butter into a large heatproof bowl and melt really slowly over a pan of just-simmering water. (We weigh ours directly into our stainless steel stand mixer bowl to minimise washing up.) Leave the melted chocolate to cool a little while you weigh out your other ingredients. Put the caster and light brown sugar into a bowl, then beat in the eggs and the vanilla extract. Weigh the plain and self-raising flours into another small bowl and add a pinch of salt.

Add the eggs and sugar to the cooled melted chocolate and mix with a spatula (or on low if you're using a mixer). The moment when the split-looking, rather grainy batter comes together into a smooth glossy bowl of loveliness is still one of my very favourite baking moments.

cont.

Add in the flours and salt and fold in gently with the spatula (or on low if you're using a mixer) until you can't see any flour – give the bottom of the bowl a good scrape just to make sure. Pour the batter into the lined traybake tin. I'm not a patient woman, so trust me when I say take some time to flatten the mixture off and make sure it's pushed well into the corners; otherwise you will end up with thin, biscuity bits.

Give the caramel a stir to loosen it a little, then dot generously heaped teaspoons all over the brownie batter, making sure there's at least one blob in every portion. Swirl the edges of each blob a wee bit with a knife. You don't want to mix in the pockets of caramel completely, but just create a swirly pattern so people can see it's got caramel in it! Bake on the middle shelf for around 25 minutes.

Assessing the baking time is really the only remotely tricky part of this recipe: if it's underbaked the brownies will be too wet and if it's over baked, you'll end up with a dry (but still tasty) chocolate cake. So, here's what we do. After 25 minutes, insert a skewer into the centre of the brownie. If there are one or two damp crumbs on the skewer, it's ready. If there's any wet batter at all, it's underdone, so put it in for five more minutes before checking again.

Leave in the tin to cool before lifting it out using the greaseproof paper. Even if you're planning to eat the brownie warm, let it sit for 15 minutes or so before cutting. It's very fragile just out of the oven.

Variations
Once you've nailed this recipe, you can use it as a base for lots of different flavours and add-ins.

SALTED CARAMEL BROWNIES
Sprinkle with a little flaked sea salt before eating.
But just a little!

RASPBERRY BROWNIES
Replace the caramel with the same amount of good raspberry jam and dot fresh raspberries over before baking (it might take a little longer to bake).

Grown-up Tiffin

We included this in the Everyday Treats section because it's so easy to whip up, but make no mistake – it really is an indulgent treat. This recipe makes a really rich, really substantial tiffin. It looks great piled up on a cake stand with candles in it as an alternative to a birthday cake.

You can make this with the Milk Chocolate 'Digestive' Biscuits on page 65 if you fancy, but the truth is that it's much better with shop-bought digestives!

- Don't stir the white chocolate chips into the base at the same time as everything else. The chocolate butter mixture is still quite warm at that stage, so by stirring in the biscuits, fruit and nuts first, you'll bring the temperature down before you add the chips, and they won't melt.

- To roast the pecans, put them on a baking tray in the oven at 180°C (160°C fan) for five to seven minutes and allow to cool.

- The base looks a little greasy when you pack it into the tin. Don't worry – that's as it should be.

- If you have to feed a crowd, double this recipe and make it in a 35 x 24cm traybake tin. This would give you 12 generous portions or 16 smaller ones.

MAKES 6–8 SLICES

23cm cake or flan tin, lined

For the base:
200g unsalted butter, cubed
150g milk chocolate,
  chips or chopped
150g dark chocolate,
  chips or chopped
50g golden syrup
300g shop-bought
  digestive biscuits
50g dried cranberries
50g pecan nuts, roasted
  and roughly chopped
50g white chocolate chips

Start with the base. Add the cubed butter, milk and dark chocolates and golden syrup into a big heatproof bowl – this is the bowl you'll end up mixing everything in, so the bigger the better. Set it over a pan of just-simmering water (a couple of inches of water is plenty; you don't want it to touch the bottom of the bowl). Leave everything to melt slowly and gently.

Take the chocolate off the heat when there are no lumps of butter left. Give it a stir and don't worry if it looks a wee bit grainy. Set to one side to cool while you get on with bashing up the digestive biscuits. We put them in a big bowl and bash them with a rolling pin; you could blitz them in a food processor but it makes more washing up and our way is quicker and more fun.

cont.

Salted Caramel Crumble Bar

I wish I could say this was our idea, but it is based on a recipe on an American baking blog that I loved the sound of. It was incredibly buttery even by our standards, so we set about making a version of our own that was closer to shortbread and filled with home-made caramel and flakes of sea salt. It's been on our menu for years now and it continues to be a best seller. We make it using our home-made caramel (page 244) but it's equally lovely with a tin of shop-bought.

- We always make the base for this in a stand mixer, but if you don't have one you could use a food processor.

- Don't leave out the salt even if you're not a big fan of salted caramel – it really helps cut the sweetness.

- This is really fragile until it's cooled, so don't lift it out of the tin before then or the base will break.

- Store in an airtight container in a cool place for up to three days.

SERVES 12

35 x 24cm traybake tin, lined

For the base and topping:
350g cold unsalted butter, cubed
200g caster sugar
150g icing sugar
1 tsp vanilla extract
550g plain flour

For the filling:
½ batch of Soft Caramel
 (page 244), completely cooled
 or 1 x 397g tin shop-bought
 caramel
½ tsp sea salt flakes

Preheat the oven to 180°C (160°C fan).

Weigh the butter, caster and icing sugars and vanilla into your stand mixer bowl and mix on low for three to four minutes until everything comes together and looks lighter in colour. It won't look light and fluffy, but that's ok.

Add the flour and mix again on low – it won't come together as a dough but will look a bit like chunky breadcrumbs. Spoon about half of the mixture into the lined traybake tin and press it down firmly to make a solid base. Bake on the middle shelf for 18 to 20 minutes until the base is starting to go golden brown in the centre. Set aside to cool.

cont.

The only bad news is that you need to leave the traybake to cool before you can drizzle it with the chocolate. Even if you want to skip the drizzling stage (though why would you?) don't be tempted to cut it up while it's still warm: the traybake will fall apart.

Once it is completely cool, gently melt the remaining 60g white chocolate either in the microwave on low in 20 second bursts or in a heatproof bowl over just-simmering water. Either way, take it off the heat when it's almost completely melted and the residual heat will do the rest. Drizzle the chocolate over the traybake and then scatter over the freeze-dried raspberries and white chocolate chips. Pop it in the fridge till the chocolate is just set. It's now ready to cut.

Variations

CARAMEL, PECAN & DARK CHOCOLATE COOKIE BAR

For something closer to the original Caramelita, replace the jam with caramel (either a tin of shop-bought or a half quantity of the recipe on page 244) and replace all the white chocolate with the same quantity of dark chocolate. Scatter over some chopped, roasted pecans before baking.

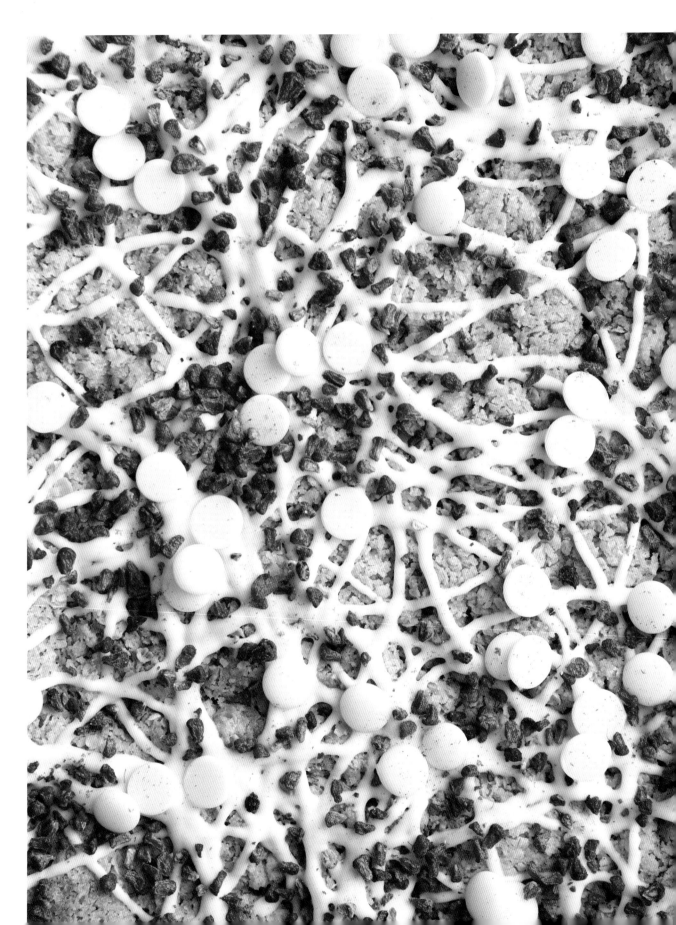

Giant Lemon Drizzles

We had some leftover vanilla batter that we didn't want to go to waste so we added lots of lemon zest to it and baked the batter in a giant muffin pan we never used. They tasted great but looked a little dull, so we covered them in a lemon glaze with a caster sugar crust and Giant Lemon Drizzles were born. They sold out immediately, so we tweaked the recipe and they've been on the menu ever since. We use an American-sized giant muffin pan and if by any chance you happen to have one, great! If you don't, you can use six large tulip wraps in a standard size muffin pan instead.

- The amount of sugar you'll need for the drizzle will depend on the juiciness of your lemons.

- These are best the day you bake them, but leftovers are fantastic toasted and topped with yoghurt and compote (see page 263).

MAKES 6

6-cup giant muffin pan or a
   standard size muffin pan
6 tulip wraps (optional)

250g unsalted butter,
   well softened (plus extra
   for greasing)
250g caster sugar
zest of 2 large lemons
5 medium eggs
1 tsp vanilla extract
275g self-raising flour

To finish:
juice of 3 lemons
approx. 200-300g caster sugar
   plus 100g more for rolling

Preheat your oven to 180°C (160°C fan) and grease the giant muffin pan really well, or pop the muffin wraps into the standard muffin pan.

Beat the butter, sugar and lemon zest together in a big mixing bowl or in your mixer until it lightens in colour and looks less dense and craggy. It won't go really fluffy but you'll see a difference after three or four minutes of mixing. Scrape down the bottom and sides of the bowl to make sure you've got all the butter mixed in.

Crack the eggs into a jug and add the vanilla and then weigh the flour into a separate bowl. Pour one egg into the creamed butter and sugar, then add a couple of spoonfuls of flour and beat until fully combined. Repeat until all the eggs are incorporated and scrape down the sides and bottom of the bowl, then gently mix in the remaining flour.

cont.

Divide the mixture between the giant muffin pan holes. Bake for 25 to 30 minutes, testing with a skewer after 25 minutes. If the skewer comes out clean, they're ready. If not pop the pan back in for another five minutes and test again: do test each cake as bake times will vary depending on where it is in the oven and how much mix is in the tin.

Leave the cakes to cool in their tins for 30 minutes before easing them out by gently running a palette knife round the sides. Place them on a cooling rack over a tray or piece of parchment. If you've used muffin wraps, carefully peel them off and place the cakes on the cooling rack as above.

For the glaze, all you do is put the lemon juice into a bowl and add the sugar till you get a glaze thick enough to coat the cake and not soak completely into it – think the consistency of single cream. Start with 200g sugar and add up to 100g more if you need to.

Dunk the top and bottom of each cake in the glaze, then roll the sides in it until completely coated. Let the excess glaze drip off into the bowl (you'll need it all), then pop the cakes back on the rack so they can drip onto the tray beneath. Don't worry if the glaze gets crumbs in it, you won't see them on the finished cakes. If you have any glaze left over, just pour it over the tops of the cakes.

Place another 100g caster sugar in a wide shallow bowl. Roll the glazed cakes in the sugar until they have a fine layer all over, then tap or brush off any excess: you just want enough to create a crunch and make the cakes look pretty. You can just do the top if you'd prefer.

Variations

GIANT LIME OR ORANGE DRIZZLES
Replace the lemons with three limes or a large orange.

Double Chocolate Muffins

These are such a favourite in the bakery. Dark, rich and chocolatey without being too sweet, the muffins are surprisingly light and fluffy and the sour cream makes it a really moist bake. It is a really simple wet-into-dry recipe and a great base recipe to have up your sleeve as you can easily mix up the flavours by using white or milk chocolate chips instead, or by replacing the chocolate with fresh raspberries or chopped fudge and pecans.

- Muffins really don't like being overmixed. If you overmix, your muffins will be a little rubbery (but they will still taste great!).

- These are best on the day they're baked but they are still lovely the next day if stored in an airtight container in a cool place.

MAKES 8 BIG MUFFINS

12-cup muffin pan
8 large tulip muffin wraps
    (see page 9)

240g self-raising flour
60g good quality cocoa powder,
    the darker the better
150g soft light brown sugar
150g caster sugar
250ml sour cream
100g unsalted butter, melted
2 medium eggs
50ml hot, strong coffee
    (or 2 heaped tsp instant
    espresso powder dissolved
    in 50ml boiling water)
150g 70% dark chocolate chips
    (or chunks)
salt

Preheat the oven to 200°C (180°C fan) and put the muffin wraps in the muffin pan. Weigh out the flour, cocoa, brown and caster sugars into a big bowl with a pinch of salt and give it a quick mix to combine. If there are lumps of brown sugar, just rub them in with your fingers as if you were making crumble.

Measure the sour cream into a jug, then add the melted butter, eggs and coffee and whisk with a fork to combine. Make sure it's well mixed as the less mixing you have to do later, the better. It will look curdled, but don't worry.

Pour the sour cream and egg mix over the dry ingredients and stir gently until the dry ingredients are nearly combined. You want to be able to see some dry flour in the batter. Add the chocolate chips and give a final gentle stir. Again, you want everything to be only just combined.

Divide the batter equally between the tulip wraps with an ice cream scoop if you have one (or a spoon if you don't) – they will seem very full.

cont.

To finish (optional):
100g 70% dark chocolate chips
   (or chunks)
25g unsalted butter

Bake on the top shelf of your oven for around 30 to 35 minutes, checking after 25 minutes with a skewer. They are ready when the skewer comes out clean and dry and the top feels springy to the touch. You might hit a chocolate chip, which will look like unbaked batter, so do test a couple of muffins to make sure.

Leave to cool in the tins for ten minutes, then transfer to a cooling rack to cool completely – though we often skip that stage and eat them warm!

If you're going to top the muffins, let them get cool and then gently melt the chocolate and butter together in the microwave (on low in 20 second bursts, stirring after each) or in a heatproof bowl over just-simmering water. Stir the mixture until it's smooth and set aside to cool and thicken slightly. Dollop a spoonful on the top of each muffin and scatter over a few more chocolate chips if you fancy.

Blueberry, Lime & Coconut Loaf

This is a lovely, summery loaf that looks very impressive but is deceptively easy. All it is is a bit of mixing! No creaming butter and sugar, just wet ingredients into dry. The loaf looks particularly pretty if, while it's still warm, you drizzle the top with lime curd and sprinkle over some curls of toasted coconut. We use the Lime Curd on page 258 but you could use shop-bought or lime marmalade or a lime drizzle.

- This cake is best on the day because of the fresh fruit, but leftovers can be refrigerated and enjoyed the next day.

- Give your tin of coconut milk a good stir to combine before you weigh out 130g.

- We use 120g yoghurt here because that's the size of the pot we buy, but if you have slightly more or less then just adjust the amount of coconut milk you use to make the combined weight 250g.

SERVES 8

2lb (23 x 13 x 7cm) loaf tin, greased and lined

240g self-raising flour
160g caster sugar
50g desiccated coconut
zest of 2 limes
3 medium eggs
2 tsp vanilla extract
120g unsalted butter, melted and cooled slightly
120g full-fat natural or Greek yoghurt
130g tinned coconut milk
200g blueberries tossed in a spoon of flour

Preheat the oven to 180°C (160°C fan).

Weigh the flour, sugar, desiccated coconut and lime zest into your mixing bowl and give it a little whisk to combine.

Mix the eggs, vanilla, melted butter, yoghurt and coconut milk in a jug (don't worry if it curdles), then pour it into the dry ingredients. Mix gently until it's almost combined (you want to see a little dry flour), then gently fold in the blueberries. Be careful not to overmix as it can make your loaf a little tough.

Spoon the batter into the lined loaf tin and smooth the top with the back of a spoon or a palette knife. The tin will look full, but don't worry – it will be just fine!

To finish (optional):
2 tbsp Lime Curd (page 258)
1 tbsp toasted coconut flakes or
    desiccated coconut
handful of fresh blueberries

Bake on the middle shelf of the oven for around 60 to 70 minutes. After 60 minutes, test the centre with a skewer, and if it doesn't come out clean pop it back in the oven for five minutes and check again (you may need to do this more than once). The top of the loaf bakes to a lovely dark colour so don't get it out too early without checking the insides are done.

Leave to cool in the tin for half an hour or so, then lift the loaf out and leave to cool completely on a wire rack.

Or, when it's still warm, paint the top of the loaf with the curd and scatter over the toasted coconut flakes and a handful of blueberries. Let the cake stand at room temperature for a wee while before you eat it.

Variations

Replace the curd with a lime drizzle: just juice one of the limes and add caster sugar until you get a thick glaze, the consistency of double cream. You don't want a thin drizzle that will soak into the cake as it will fall apart.

Replace the limes with two lemons for a Blueberry, Lemon and Coconut Loaf.

Cranberry, Almond & Yoghurt Loaf

This loaf is a favourite at Christmas time; packed with flavour, it looks lovely just as it is and doesn't need any decorating to look festive. It's also really easy, which makes it the perfect festive bake. It's not just for Christmas though: you can use raspberries instead of fresh cranberries to make it the rest of the year.

- If you're using raspberries, don't dot them over the top of the loaf before baking as they will burn.

- When you're testing the loaf, bear in mind you might hit a chunk of marzipan which can look like wet batter. Give your skewer a wipe and try another spot.

SERVES 6–8

2lb (23 x 13 x 7cm) loaf tin, lined

240g self-raising flour
160g caster sugar
3 medium eggs
120g unsalted butter, melted and cooled slightly
250g full-fat natural or Greek yoghurt
2 tsp vanilla extract
120g fresh cranberries (or frozen, defrosted), tossed in a spoon of flour
120g marzipan, chopped into 1cm cubes and tossed in a spoon of flour
salt

Preheat the oven to 180°C (160°C fan).

Weigh the flour and sugar into your mixing bowl and add a pinch of salt. Give it a little mix to combine.

Mix the eggs, melted butter, yoghurt and vanilla in a jug (don't worry if it looks curdled), then pour it onto the flour and sugar. Mix gently till everything's almost combined (you want to see a little dried flour), then gently fold in the cranberries and marzipan until just combined. Be careful not to overmix as it can make your loaf a little tough.

Spoon the batter into your lined loaf tin and smooth the top with the back of a spoon or a palette knife. Sprinkle over the flaked almonds and, if you like, dot more fresh cranberries over the top, pushing them into the batter just a little so they don't move. The tin will look pretty full but the loaf doesn't rise much.

To finish:
20g flaked almonds
handful of fresh cranberries
(optional)

Bake on the middle shelf of the oven for around 60 to 70 minutes. If it looks like the top is getting too dark mid-bake, cover with a piece of baking paper folded over the tin. After 60 minutes, test the centre with a skewer, and if it doesn't come out clean pop it back in the oven for five minutes and check again (you may need to do this more than once). The outside does bake to a lovely dark colour but inside will have a lovely moist, light crumb.

Leave the loaf to cool in the tin for half an hour or so, then lift it using the overhang of baking paper and leave to cool, still in the paper, on a cooling rack.

Chocolate, Banana & Coconut Loaf

V

This is a lovely, slightly squidgy, very chocolatey loaf which just happens to be vegan. The predominant flavour is chocolate and a hint of banana, the coconut milk provides a richness and the desiccated coconut gives it a nice nubbly texture. Whether you are vegan or not, if you're a fan of very chocolatey and moist cake, this is one for you!

- Coconut milk often separates in the tin so give it a good stir to mix before you measure it out.

- Make sure you weigh the banana: it's acting as an egg substitute to bind the cake so the quantities are important.

- This loaf is very fragile when freshly baked, so allow some time for it to stand before you take it out of the tin. It is actually better on day two when it will have firmed up and the flavours have fully developed.

SERVES 8–10

2lb (23 x 13 x 7cm) loaf tin, lined

230g self-raising flour
160g caster sugar
160g soft light brown sugar
60g good quality dark
    cocoa powder
1 tsp baking powder
250ml tinned coconut milk
90g unsalted plant-based butter,
    melted (or same weight
    of vegetable oil)
110ml soya or other plant-based
    milk
130g very ripe banana,
    well mashed
60g desiccated coconut

Preheat the oven to 180°C (160°C) fan.

Weigh the flour, caster and soft brown sugars, cocoa and baking powder into your mixing bowl and give it a little mix to combine. (If you're using a mixer, make sure it's on low.)

Put the coconut milk in a jug with the melted butter or vegetable oil, soya milk and mashed banana. Mix with a fork, then pour it over the dry ingredients and mix gently until completely combined. Scrape down the sides and bottom of the bowl with a spatula to make sure you've mixed in all the dry ingredients. Finally, stir in the desiccated coconut.

cont.

To finish:

juice of 2 clementines
    or ½ an orange
approx. 150–250g caster sugar
50g roasted hazelnuts,
    roughly chopped (optional)

Spoon the batter into the greased, lined tin and flatten it off using an angled palette knife or the back of a spoon. Bake on the middle shelf for around 50 to 55 minutes and then check to see if it's ready with a skewer. If not, bake for another five minutes and check again.

While the cake's baking, make the drizzle for the top. Mix the clementine juice with 150g caster sugar: you want a thick, crunchy glaze that will pour and spread but won't disappear completely into the cake. Add more sugar if it's not thick enough: ours is the consistency of thick double cream.

Let the cake cool in its tin for 20 minutes, then pour over the glaze. When the glaze is almost set, scatter chopped roasted hazelnuts round the outer edge of the cake. If you do it too soon they will sink into the glaze, too late and the glaze will set and they won't stick. Leave to fully set before you take the cake out of the tin. You can use a palette knife to loosen round the edges.

Variation

CLEMENTINE, CINNAMON & HAZELNUT CAKE
Replace the cardamom with ground cinnamon.

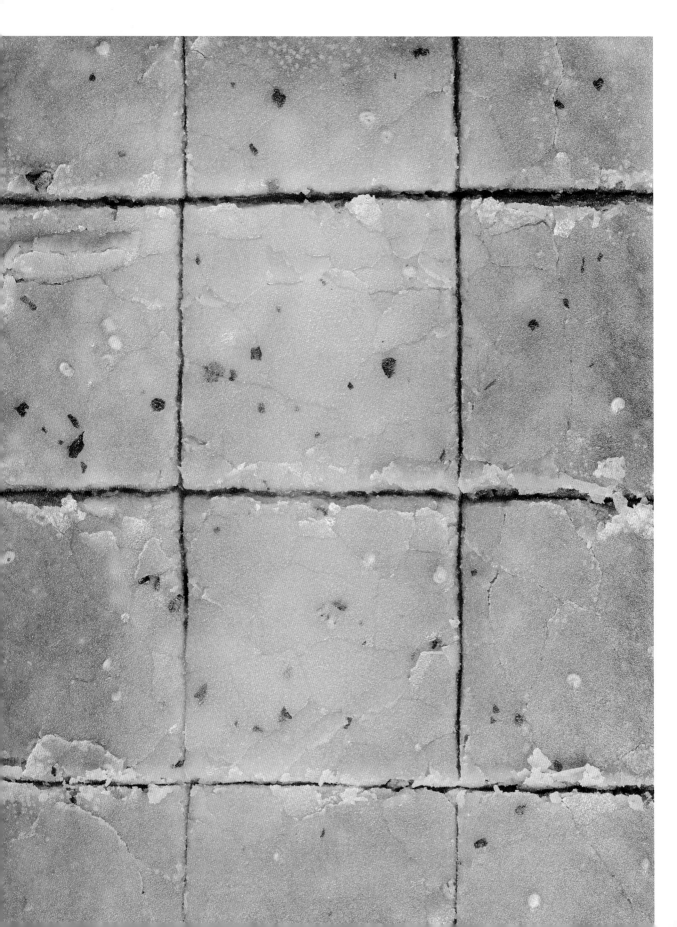

Coconut, Chilli & Lime Cake

This cake doesn't look like much, but don't let that fool you. It's packed full of flavour, incredibly easy to make and is a great favourite at the bakery – we put it on the counter when it's still warm and it always flies out. There's something really satisfying about serving warm cake.

- If your coconut milk has separated, tip it into a bowl and give it a whisk – it doesn't matter if it's a bit lumpy.

- This keeps well, covered, for up to three days, and leftovers are delicious warmed up in the microwave.

- Adding the chilli flakes just before the second glaze means that the top of the traybake will be flecked with red. It not only looks pretty and adds to the flavour, but it also gives people a wee warning about the chilli. That said, the cake isn't fiery at all so if you like things hotter feel free to add a little more chilli.

SERVES 12

35 x 24cm traybake tin, lined

525g self-raising flour
450g soft light brown sugar
50g desiccated coconut
1½ tsp baking powder
½ tsp chilli flakes
½ tsp salt
zest of 4 limes
400ml soya milk
100ml vegetable oil
150ml tinned coconut milk
1 tsp vanilla extract

To finish:
juice of 2 limes
approx. 150–250g caster sugar
¼ tsp chilli flakes

Preheat the oven to 180°C (160°C fan).

Weigh the flour, sugar, coconut, baking powder, chilli flakes, salt and lime zest into a big mixing bowl. Give it a quick whisk (on low if you're using a mixer) to combine.

Measure out the soya milk and pour it over the dry ingredients, then do the same with the vegetable oil. Stir the coconut milk before you measure it and add it to the bowl too along with the vanilla. Gently whisk the batter until it's smooth and you can't see any dry bits of flour; scrape round the bowl with a spatula to make sure it's all mixed in.

Pour the batter into the lined traybake tin and bake on the middle shelf for about 40 to 45 minutes. Test with a skewer after 40 minutes – it's ready when the skewer comes out clean.

cont.

Let the cake cool for 15 minutes or so in the tin while you get on with making the glaze. All you do is put the lime juice in a bowl and add enough sugar to give you a thick glaze that will pour and spread but won't disappear completely into the cake. Start with 150g sugar and add more if you need to. Ours is the consistency of runny honey. You want it to set on the top of the cake to make a nice crunchy, sugary crust as well as adding lots of flavour.

Skewer the cake all over to create little holes for the glaze to drip into. Pour over about half the glaze and, using a pastry brush, spread it over the top of the cake and leave to soak in for about ten minutes. Stir the chilli flakes into the remaining glaze and spread over once the cake has cooled a little more (it doesn't have to be completely cool).

Serve still warm.

Date, Apple & Walnut Cake

This cake started its life as a sticky toffee cake, but we had some apples to spare and set about experimenting and here is the result! It's a really simple cake to make, but somehow the rows of apple slices on the top make it look much fancier than it really is. The apple jelly glaze intensifies the flavours and gives the apple slices a lovely shine.

- Feel free to leave the walnuts out if you'd prefer, or replace them with the same amount of pecans or hazelnuts.

- This cake is at its best on the day it's made, but it will be fine for another day or so if you keep it in an airtight container in the fridge. It's delicious gently warmed in the microwave on day two.

SERVES 9–12

32 x 21cm traybake tin, lined

150g chopped dried dates
150ml apple juice
250g unsalted butter, softened
275g soft light brown sugar
5 medium eggs
280g self-raising flour
1 tbsp ground cinnamon
½ tsp baking powder
1 small red apple, skin on,
    cored and grated

Preheat the oven to 180°C (160°C) fan.

Put the chopped dates and apple juice in a small pan on a medium heat and simmer until the liquid is almost all absorbed. Set aside to cool.

Put the softened butter and sugar in your bowl or stand mixer and beat until it looks lighter in colour and less craggy. Crack your eggs into a jug and weigh the flour, cinnamon and baking powder into another bowl.

Pour one egg into the butter and sugar and add a spoonful of flour. Mix (on low if you're using a mixer) until fully combined, then repeat with each of the remaining eggs. Add the rest of the flour and mix till it's just combined.

cont.

To finish:

3 small red apples, skin on, halved, cored and thinly sliced

4 tbsp Apple Jelly (page 252) or apricot jam (optional)

75g walnuts, roughly chopped

You'll need to scrape the sides and bottom of the bowl with a spatula after each addition. Stir in the cooled date mixture and the grated apple with a spatula until combined, and spoon into the lined tin, smoothing the batter out with a palette knife or the back of a spoon. Neatly arrange the sliced apples in rows across the top.

Bake on the middle shelf of the oven for 60 to 65 minutes. Test the centre with a skewer after an hour, and if it doesn't come out clean pop back in the oven for five minutes, then check again. (You may need to do this more than once – every oven is different, so don't worry if yours takes a bit longer to bake.)

Leave to cool in the tin for 15 minutes or so while you make the glaze (if you're using it). Pop the apple jelly and two tablespoons of water in a very small pan and put over a low heat until it begins to boil (you can also do it in a microwave on low). Stir until it's smooth and then glaze the top of the warm cake with it using a pastry brush. Scatter over the chopped walnuts while the glaze is still warm.

Leave to cool a little in the tin before lifting out using the paper and slicing.

Coconut & Lime Drizzle Cake

This zingy, slightly tropical drizzle cake is perfect for a summer party. Don't let the fact that it's gluten-free put you off – it's a really tasty, light cake and it's very simple to make.

- Don't leave out the xanthan gum: it stops the cake crumbling and falling apart when you cut it. Don't overmix it as the gum can make the batter a bit gluey.

- Test to see if the cake is ready with a skewer and don't go by timings alone. If the top is looking a little dark when you first test it, loosely cover the top with foil.

SERVES 8–10

23cm springform cake tin, greased and lined

300g caster sugar
300g unsalted butter, softened
zest of 3 limes
6 medium eggs
150g gluten-free self-raising flour
1 tsp xanthan gum
150g desiccated coconut

To finish:
juice of 3 limes
approx. 250g caster sugar
10g desiccated coconut or 25g coconut flakes, lightly toasted

Preheat the oven to 180°C (160°C fan).

Weigh the sugar and butter into your mixing bowl and add the zest. Beat together until it begins to lighten in colour (mix on medium if you're using a mixer). Scrape down the sides of the bowl with a spatula and mix again for a minute or so. Crack the eggs into a jug (don't whisk them). Weigh the flour and xanthan gum into another bowl and whisk to combine.

Pour in an egg from the jug and add a generous spoonful of flour. Beat until it's incorporated (on low if you're using a mixer). Repeat with each of the remaining eggs and then fold in any remaining flour. You may need to scrape down the sides of the bowl again. Stir in the desiccated coconut, give the bowl a final scrape down and spoon the batter into the greased and lined tin, flattening it off using a palette knife or the back of a spoon.

Bake on the middle shelf for around 50 to 55 minutes and then check with a skewer to see if it's done. If it's not, bake for another five minutes and check again.

cont.

Make the drizzle by mixing the lime juice with the caster sugar. You want a thick, crunchy sugar glaze that will add texture as well as flavour – you might need to add more sugar if your limes are very juicy.

Let the cake cool in its tin for 20 minutes, then pour over the glaze. When it's almost set, scatter toasted coconut round the outer edge of the cake. If you do it too soon, the coconut will sink into the glaze, too late and the glaze will set and the coconut won't stick. Leave to fully set before you take the cake out of the tin. Run a palette knife round the edge first to loosen the cake.

Variation

COCONUT & LEMON DRIZZLE CAKE
Replace the lime zest with the zest of two lemons and use the juice to make the drizzle.

Parsnip, Apple & Hazelnut Cake

This cake is the result of playing around with a carrot cake recipe. We wanted something that would appeal to carrot cake lovers but that was autumnal in flavour and this fits the bill. It's much lighter than it sounds and to be honest you would have no idea it has parsnips in it. It just tastes nutty and cinnamony with sweetness, moisture and texture from the apples and parsnips. Delicious.

- Take care when blitzing the nuts for the batter. If you over-blitz them, you'll end up with a paste. If you're chopping them by hand, make sure they are as fine as you can manage. You don't want big chunks of nut in the cake.

- Don't take the cake out of the tin while it's hot as it's still fragile and might break.

23cm springform cake tin, greased and lined

275g soft light brown sugar
250g unsalted butter, softened
5 medium eggs
280g self-raising flour
1½ tsp cinnamon
1 tsp baking powder
125g peeled parsnip, grated (around 1 medium-sized parsnip)
125g apples, skin on, grated (around 2 small apples)
100g hazelnuts, roasted and blitzed or very finely chopped

Preheat the oven to 180°C (160°C fan).

Weigh the sugar and butter into a large bowl and crack the eggs into a jug (don't whisk them). Weigh the flour, cinnamon and baking powder into another bowl and whisk to combine.

Beat the butter and sugar together until they look paler in colour, then scrape down the sides and bottom of the bowl with a spatula and mix again (on medium if you're using a stand mixer). Pour in an egg along with a generous spoonful of the flour and beat (on low if you're using a mixer) until it's all combined. Repeat with each of the remaining eggs, then scrape the bowl down again and gently mix in the remaining flour.

cont.

For the buttercream:
1 x loaf batch of Basic Buttercream
    (page 233)
2 tbsp hazelnut or maple syrup
50g hazelnuts, roasted roughly
    chopped (optional)

Fold in the grated parsnips, apples and blitzed nuts until they are just combined and no more. Spoon the batter into the lined tin and flatten it off using a palette knife or the back of a spoon.

Bake on the middle shelf for around 70 to 75 minutes and then check with a skewer: the cake is ready when the skewer comes out clean and dry and the middle is firm to the touch. If there's any give at all, bake for another five minutes and check again.

Leave to cool in the tin until it's just slightly warm and cool enough to handle. Then, take the cake out of the tin and gently turn it upside down on a cooling rack, take off the base of the tin and the greaseproof paper, then turn it the right way up again. It may feel very slightly damp on the bottom (just because it's been cooling in the tin), but this will go once it's cooled completely.

If you're icing the cake, make the Basic Buttercream (see page 233), and when it's very soft and smooth beat in the hazelnut or maple syrup. Ice the cake using a piping bag and palette knife or, for a more rustic look, simply use a spatula to spread a thick layer on the top of the cake. Finish with a scattering of chopped roasted hazelnuts.

Variation
For a plainer cake, brush the top with three to four tablespoons of maple syrup, or apple jelly that you've brought to the boil with two tablespoons of water.
Finish with a scattering of chopped roasted hazelnuts.

Not-S
Every
Treats

If you're looking for big, generous cakes and bakes, then this is the chapter for you! It's no surprise that most of our biggest sellers are here.

These recipes are a little more time-consuming as they tend to have toppings or a couple of stages in the method. Don't let that put you off though. The Giant Chocolate Chip Cookies or Deluxe Coconut Brownie are pretty simple to make but have earned their place here because they are so indulgent.

Recipes like the Deluxe Dipped Marshmallow Biscuits or the Pink Grapefruit Meringue Shortbread Tarts have a few stages to them, but none of them are at all difficult, we promise.

We've included cakes – like the Chocolate Raspberry Loaf or the Spiced Carrot, Pecan & Cranberry Cake – that would work for a celebration or a smaller party. They're so pretty and impressive they would be equally at home in the Celebration Cakes chapter. And last but definitely not least, our Millionaire Shortbreads get a section of their own. They are the poster child for this chapter: definitely indulgent and rich enough to be a very occasional treat, a bit of a labour of love, but not at all difficult. If you've steered clear of making your own caramel in the past, do give one of these recipes a go: the caramel is actually really easy to make and it's incredibly satisfying too.

O-
day
s

Deluxe Dipped Marshmallow Biscuits

These biscuits are our take on s'mores, the happy result of leftover Meringue Frosting and leftover digestive biscuits from the recipe on page 65. The recipe has three stages, but none of them are at all complicated, and the Meringue Frosting that fills the biscuits is a great recipe to have up your sleeve.

- The Meringue Frosting on page 243 is the only recipe in the book that requires a thermometer, and while we are all for really simple recipes with the least amount of equipment, it's really important to get the temperature right here. If you don't have a thermometer, just replace the frosting with toasted marshmallows instead.

- These biscuits must be eaten on the day if you're using the Meringue Frosting. If you need them to last a little longer, fill with toasted marshmallows instead and they'll last up to three days in an airtight container.

MAKES 8 BISCUIT SANDWICHES

7cm scone or cookie cutter
2 large baking sheets, lined

For the biscuits:
50g caster sugar (we use Vanilla Sugar, page 17)
100g unsalted butter, straight from the fridge, cubed
150g plain wholemeal flour (plus a little extra for dusting)
½ tsp baking powder
2–3 tsp milk
salt

Preheat the oven to 180°C (160°C fan).

If you're using a food processor, all you need to do is whizz together the sugar, butter, flour, baking powder and a pinch of salt until the mixture looks like breadcrumbs and there are no big lumps of butter. Tip the mix into a big bowl. If you're doing it by hand, just rub in the butter with your fingertips – it will take a bit longer. Give the bowl a shake and any rogue lumps of butter will come to the top – rub them in too.

When you have your breadcrumb-like mix in your bowl, add two teaspoons of milk and work it in using your fingers until everything starts coming together to form a crumbly dough. If you need to, add another teaspoon of milk. Form the dough into a ball: it will look crumbly and you might think there's no way it will come together, but it will.

cont.

For the filling:
1 batch of Meringue Frosting
    (page 243) or 8 large or 16
    standard marshmallows

To finish:
200g milk chocolate

Dust your work surface with a little flour and flatten your ball of dough into a disc. Roll it out to the thickness of a pound coin, moving the dough around a little on your work surface to stop it sticking.

Cut out 16 biscuits – you'll need to re-roll the dough a couple of times to get all 16. Space them out on the lined baking trays and prick each biscuit all over with a fork.

Bake for 18 to 20 minutes, until the biscuits are a dark golden brown (a little more so round the edges). They won't be firm to the touch, but they will harden as they cool. Leave to cool completely on the trays while you get on with making the Meringue Frosting on page 243.

Either pipe a generous dome of frosting on eight of the biscuits or place on the marshmallows. Place the topped biscuits on a baking tray and put under a very hot grill. Watch them like a hawk as you want the meringue or marshmallow to be lightly scorched, not burnt. You can use a blowtorch for this stage, but to be honest we are all a little scared of the blowtorch and just use the grill!

Melt the chocolate in a small, deep, heatproof bowl either in a microwave or over a small pan of barely simmering water.

Take each of the remaining biscuits and dot a little blob of the melted chocolate on the underside. Place each, chocolate-side down, on top of the toasted meringue or marshmallow and give it a little press to make sure it sticks.

Next, dip the biscuits in the remaining melted chocolate (you need the melted chocolate to be deep enough to cover half the biscuit in one dunk). Dunk each of the biscuits so they are half covered and put them on a lined baking tray in the fridge for five minutes or so to set.

Giant Chocolate Chip Cookies

This recipe is all thanks to our Head Baker, Toni. These cookies are her babies and she makes them most mornings – we put them out on the counter still warm and the smell in the café is amazing. Hard to describe, they have a bit of a crust on the outside but the insides are soft and cakey and packed full of chocolate.

- Feel free to vary the chocolate chips. You can use all milk, white or dark chocolate, or try the Caramelised White Chocolate on page 249.

- You can freeze the unbaked cookies and defrost them overnight in the fridge. Take them out of the fridge and let them sit at room temperature for 15 minutes before baking.

- We make big 150g cookies, but if you want to make smaller ones reduce the baking time accordingly.

- These are fantastic warm, just out of the oven, and at their best on the day of baking. They will keep for two days in a cool place if you wrap them in cling film and store in an airtight container. On day two, try warming them up in the microwave or make Hot Mess (page 263).

MAKES 8 GIANT COOKIES

2 baking sheets, lined

175g plain flour
175g strong white bread flour
75g cornflour
1 tsp salt
½ tsp baking powder
5 medium egg yolks
150g milk chocolate chips
    or chunks
150g white chocolate chips
    or chunks

Preheat the oven to 180°C (160°C fan).

Weigh your plain flour, bread flour and cornflour into a bowl with the salt and baking powder and stir to combine. Put the egg yolks in a jug (you can freeze the whites to make the Meringue Frosting on page 243). Weigh the chocolate chips or chunks into a small bowl.

Cream the butter with the sugar and vanilla in your mixing bowl until the mix lightens in colour and looks less craggy. This takes minutes with a stand or hand-held mixer, but it will take a little longer with a mixing bowl and a spoon.

cont.

150g unsalted butter, softened
220g soft light brown sugar
1 tsp vanilla extract
1–2 tbsp milk (optional)

Scrape your bowl down and give it another mix, then add the flours and the egg yolks at the same time. Mix (on low if you're using a mixer) until everything is combined, scraping the bowl down as you go. Lastly, add in the chocolate chips and mix again until they are mixed through. The mixture will look like rubble – if it doesn't, add one or two tablespoons of milk.

Divide this rubble into eight portions. The easiest way to do this is by weight: for each one, take 150g and squeeze it into a ball. Place the balls on your lined baking sheet and pop in the fridge to chill for ten minutes.

Bake for 25 minutes, then check the cookies. They are ready when they are golden brown and the middles feel set and firm-ish to the touch – if they're too soft, pop them back in the oven for a few minutes more. You want them to be soft but not gooey when baked.

Leave the cookies to cool on the baking sheet for ten minutes if you want to eat them still warm, or transfer to a wire rack to cool completely.

S'mores Brownie Cups

This recipe came about because we had some Meringue Frosting to use up and it's become a firm favourite. The cup part is a cross between a sponge cake and a brownie and it's super simple to make. If you don't have a thermometer to make Meringue Frosting, you can use giant marshmallows instead.

- It's worth taking the time to grease the tin well and dust each one with cocoa. Otherwise, the cakes tend to stick to the tin and break when you try to take them out.

- The Meringue Frosting on page 243 is the only recipe in the book that requires a thermometer, and while we are all for really simple recipes with the least amount of equipment, it's really important to get the temperature right here.

- If you don't have a thermometer, replace the frosting with toasted marshmallows instead.

- If you're using the Meringue Frosting these are only good on the day they are made, but if you use toasted marshmallows store them in a cool place in an airtight container and they'll be fine the next day.

MAKES 10

12-hole muffin tin with 10 of the holes really well greased with butter and dusted with cocoa

175g good quality 70% dark chocolate, chips or chopped
150g unsalted butter, chopped
100g caster sugar
100g soft light brown sugar
3 medium eggs
1 tsp vanilla extract
75g self-raising flour
¼ tsp baking powder
salt

Preheat the oven to 180°C (160°C fan).

Weigh your chocolate and butter into a large heatproof bowl and melt really slowly over a pan of just-simmering water. We weigh ours directly into our stainless steel stand mixer bowl. Leave to cool.

Weigh the caster and brown sugars into a bowl, then break in the eggs and add the vanilla. Weigh the flour, baking powder and a pinch of salt into another small bowl. Mix the eggs and sugar into the cooled melted chocolate with a spatula (or on low if you're using a mixer). Then gently fold in the flour until everything is combined. Give the bottom of the bowl a good scrape with the spatula to make sure there are no pockets of flour.

cont.

To finish:
1 batch of Meringue Frosting
   (page 243) or 10 giant/20
   standard marshmallows
3–4 tbsp Soft Caramel (page 244)
   or use shop-bought (optional)
1 digestive biscuit, crushed into
   crumbs (optional)

Divide the mixture equally between the ten greased and dusted muffin holes. Bake on the middle shelf for 20 to 25 minutes, checking with a skewer after 20 minutes. If there are one or two damp crumbs on the skewer, they're ready. If there's any wet batter at all, pop them back in the oven for another five minutes and check again.

Leave in the tin to cool before carefully lifting each cup out using a palette knife. Place them on a baking tray while you get on with the Meringue Frosting (page 243). Either spoon the frosting into a piping bag with an open-tip nozzle and pipe a generous dome onto the top of each one or, for a more rough and ready finish, spoon a mound on each cup and smooth it over with a palette knife. If you're not making the Meringue Frosting, place a marshmallow or two on each brownie cup.

Put the baking tray of cups under a very hot grill to toast the tops. Watch them like a hawk though! When they are scorched but not burned, they are ready. Drizzle or pipe the caramel over the toasted meringue and sprinkle with digestive crumbs.

Variations
For Caramel S'mores Brownie Cups, put a generous spoonful of caramel on top of the batter before baking.

Pink Grapefruit Meringue Shortbread Tarts

We love these light, citrusy, indulgent tarts. We fill them with a thick layer of home-made Grapefruit Curd (page 258), which has a beautiful soft peachy colour, but it works just as well with lime or lemon curd, home-made or shop-bought. The tart shells are incredibly easy to make: there's no pastry or rolling out; it's just a thick layer of shortbread dough pressed into individual pie tins.

· The Meringue Frosting is the only recipe in the book that requires a thermometer. If you don't have one, you can top each tart with a shop-bought meringue instead.

· Because of the Meringue Frosting, these tarts must be eaten on the day so we usually top them just before serving. The unfilled shells will keep in an airtight container in a cool place for up to three days.

MAKES 6 TARTS

6 x 10cm pie tins or individual tart tins with removable bases

For the tart shells:
175g unsalted butter, cold and cubed
100g caster sugar
75g icing sugar
1 tsp vanilla extract
zest of ½ grapefruit
275g plain flour

To finish:
1 batch of Grapefruit Curd (page 258)
2 batches of Meringue Frosting (page 243) or 6 shop-bought meringues

Preheat the oven to 180°C (160°C fan). Weigh the butter, caster and icing sugars, vanilla and grapefruit zest into the mixer bowl or processor and mix until everything comes together and looks a bit lighter in colour. Add the flour and mix on low until you have what looks a bit like breadcrumbs – it won't come together as a dough.

Divide the mixture into six and press into each of the tins, working it up the sides to create a tart shell that's an even thickness all over. Put on a baking tray and bake for 25 to 30 minutes until the shells are light golden brown all over. Set aside to cool while you make the Meringue Frosting on page 243.

Once the shells are cool, take them out of the tins and fill each one with a layer of curd. We like ours almost filled to the top, but you can use as little or as much as you fancy. Next, dollop or pipe a generous dome of Meringue Frosting on top of each tart. Put the tarts on a baking tray under a very hot grill to toast – watch them like a hawk as you want them lightly scorched, not burnt – or alternatively give them a blast with a kitchen blowtorch. Serve immediately.

Spiced Carrot, Pecan & Cranberry Cake

This isn't your average carrot cake: it's a deep, dark cake jam-packed with carrots, nuts and cranberries, as rich as a Christmas fruit cake. The chai spice mix gives it a little background hint of heat. You can dress this cake up or down; while it's lovely as it is or simply glazed with some marmalade, it has earned its place in this chapter because we top it with orange buttercream, dried cranberries and pecans.

· Keep any left over chai spice mix in a jar with a lid to give a bit of spice to biscuits, tea or hot chocolate. Use the same quantity of cinnamon if you'd rather.

· Roast the pecans on an unlined baking tray in the oven at 180°C (160°C fan) for five to seven minutes.

SERVES 8–10

23cm springform cake tin, bottom and sides lined with baking paper and the outside wrapped in foil

For the chai spice mix:
3 tsp ground cinnamon
1 tsp ground cardamom
1 tsp ground ginger
½ tsp allspice
½ tsp ground cloves
¼ tsp ground nutmeg

For the cake:
275g soft dark brown sugar
250ml vegetable oil
5 medium eggs
250g carrots, peeled and grated
150g dried cranberries

Preheat the oven to 180°C (160°C fan).

First, make the chai spice mix – just mix the cinnamon, cardamom, ginger, allspice, cloves and nutmeg in a small bowl.

Put the sugar, oil and eggs in a large bowl and set aside. Put the carrots, cranberries, chopped pecan nuts and orange zest in another bowl. Weigh the flour, chai spice mix and baking powder into a third bowl and give it a little mix to combine.

All you need to do now is a bit of mixing. Beat the eggs, sugar and oil until well combined and a little frothy, then stir in the carrots, cranberries, pecans and orange zest. Finally, fold in the flour mix until there are no dry bits of flour and pour the whole lot in the prepared tin.

Place the cake tin on a baking tray on the middle shelf of the oven and bake for about 70 to 75 minutes but check with a skewer after 65. If it doesn't come out clean, pop the tin back in and check again after five minutes (you may need to do this more than once).

cont.

75g pecan nuts, roasted
    and finely chopped
zest of 1 large orange
280g self-raising flour
4 tsp chai spice mix or 2 tsp
    ground cinnamon
1 tsp baking powder

To finish:
1 x loaf batch of Basic Buttercream
    (page 233)
zest of 1 large orange
20 pecan nuts, roasted
a handful of dried cranberries
    (optional)

Leave to cool for half an hour or so in the tin, then take the cake out and leave to cool completely on a cooling rack. Remove the paper once the cake is completely cool.

While it's cooling, beat the orange zest into your Basic Buttercream until it's thoroughly mixed in. Use a piping bag and an open nozzle to pipe the icing in a thick layer on the top of the cake and smooth with a palette knife. Scatter the pecans and cranberries round the edge.

Variation
To glaze with marmalade, mix four tablespoons of marmalade with a tablespoon of water and microwave on high till it begins to boil. Give it a mix and, using a pastry brush, paint the top of the cake with it. You can still scatter over the cranberries and pecans if you fancy.

Cakes

Bakes

Burgers

Breakfast

offee

viches

Sticky Toffee Pecan Slice

Imagine a cross between a sticky toffee pudding and a sponge cake. This is it! It's lighter than a traditional sticky toffee pudding, but it still has all the flavour and it makes a lovely autumn pudding served warm, straight out of the oven, and topped with Brown Sugar Glaze. It's equally lovely served at room temperature, like we do in the bakery.

- Roast the pecans on an unlined baking tray in the oven at 180°C (160°C fan) for five to seven minutes.

- You can use apple juice instead of Earl Grey tea to cook the dates.

- The unglazed cake will last up to three days if you keep it in an airtight container in a cool place. If you're going to eat it over a couple of days, just glaze the slices as you need them and keep the leftover glaze in the fridge (it will last up to three days too).

SERVES 9–12

32 x 21cm traybake tin, lined

200g chopped dried dates
200ml hot, strong Earl Grey tea
   made with one teabag
250g unsalted butter, softened
300g soft dark brown sugar
6 medium eggs
300g self-raising flour
1 tsp baking powder
100g pecan nuts, roasted
   and finely chopped

To finish:
1 batch of Brown Sugar Glaze
   (page 248)
24 pecan nuts, roasted

Preheat the oven to 180°C (160°C) fan.

Put the chopped dates in a small pan with the Earl Grey tea and simmer on a medium heat until the liquid is absorbed and you're left with a sticky mixture. Set aside to cool while you get on with the rest of the cake.

Next put the softened butter and sugar in your mixing bowl and beat until the mixture starts to look lighter in colour and less craggy. Crack your eggs into a jug and weigh the flour and baking powder into another bowl.

Pour one egg into the creamed butter and sugar along with a spoonful of flour and beat until everything is combined. Repeat with each of the remaining eggs, then fold in the rest of the flour until it's just combined. You'll need to scrape the sides and bottom of the bowl with a spatula after each addition.

Add the cooled date mixture and the chopped pecans and mix thoroughly with a spatula. Spoon into the lined tin, smoothing it out with a palette knife or the back of a spoon.

cont.

Bake on the middle shelf of the oven for around 50 to 55 minutes. After 50 minutes, test the centre with a skewer, and if it doesn't come out clean pop the tin back in the oven for five minutes before checking again (you may need to do this more than once). This cake does bake dark because of the brown sugar, so don't let that fool you into thinking it's ready!

If you're eating this as a pudding, warm from the oven, pour the glaze over the top and scatter over the pecans, then serve straight from the tin. If you're having it at room temperature, let the cake cool in the tin until just warm, then take it out and slice it and glaze each slice on the plate. The glaze will drip down the sides. Finish each slice with a couple of pecans on top. Lovely!

Chocolate, Coconut & Pecan Cake

This cake is inspired by the flavours in German chocolate cake, but the topping – a thick layer of crunchy, nutty coconut and soft caramel – takes centre stage. The cake itself is very simple and a really versatile recipe, and the topping just takes a little mixing, but the end result is very impressive. If you don't like coconut, you could top it with the chocolate glaze on page 246 or with a simple buttercream (see page 238).

- To roast the desiccated coconut and the pecans, put them on separate baking trays in the oven at 180°C (160°C fan) for five to seven minutes.

- This cake will last for two days if stored in an airtight container in a cool place. The topping might be a little drier on day two but it will still be delicious.

SERVES 8–10

23cm springform cake tin, bottom and sides lined with baking paper and the outside wrapped in foil

320g self-raising flour
200g caster sugar
200g soft light brown sugar
80g good quality cocoa powder
100ml strong, hot coffee
300ml evaporated milk
130g unsalted butter, melted
3 medium eggs
salt

To finish:
1 x 397g can shop-bought caramel
300g desiccated coconut, roasted
150g pecans, roasted
 and finely chopped

Preheat the oven to 180°C (160°C) fan.

Weigh the flour, caster and soft brown sugars, cocoa and a pinch of salt into your mixing bowl and give it a little mix to combine. If you're using a mixer, make sure it's on low.

Next mix the coffee, evaporated milk, melted butter and eggs together, then pour them onto the flour and sugar mixture, mixing gently until everything is completely combined. Give the bottom of the bowl a good scrape with a spatula to make sure you've caught all the dry ingredients.

Pour the batter into the lined and wrapped cake tin, then pop the tin on a large baking tray (just in case there are any drips) and bake on the middle shelf for around 70 minutes. Test it with a skewer after an hour: if the skewer doesn't come out clean, pop the tin back in the oven and keep testing every five minutes until it does.

cont.

Leave the cake in the tin to cool completely. When the cake is cool, take it out of the tin and peel off the baking paper on the bottom and sides. With a serrated knife, cut off the domed top of the cake so you're left with a smooth, flat surface of soft cake. Spread three tablespoons of the tinned caramel over it. (Don't throw the cut-off cake away though! Stick it in the freezer so you can make the Cake Truffles on page 271 another day.)

Mix the rest of the caramel with the toasted coconut and chopped pecans to make a thick paste and then spread this on top of the cake. If you want a super neat finish, clip the ring part of the springform tin back around the cake to create a collar and that will help you spread the topping neatly to the edges.

Chocolate Raspberry Loaf

The combination of dark chocolate and raspberries is always a winner. In this loaf we put puréed raspberries in the chocolate cake and add pops of flavour from some freeze-dried raspberries on top. It bakes beautifully with a very satisfying crack across the top. The result is a lovely, impressive cake, perfect when you want something smaller than a layer cake for a celebration.

· The fresh fruit topping means this is really only good on the day, but you can make the loaf itself a day in advance. Wrap it in cling film and store in a cool place overnight before icing and eating the next day.

SERVES 8–10

2lb (23 x 13 x 7cm) loaf tin, lined

100g raspberries
230g self-raising flour
160g caster sugar
160g soft light brown sugar
60g good quality dark
   cocoa powder
285ml evaporated milk
90g unsalted butter, melted
2 medium eggs
salt

For the buttercream:
1 loaf batch of Basic Buttercream
   (see page 233)
165g 70% dark chocolate

Preheat the oven to 180°C (160°C fan).

Mash the raspberries really well using a fork, then push them through a sieve over a bowl so you get a lovely purée with no seeds in it.

Weigh the flour, caster and soft brown sugars and cocoa into your mixing bowl and add a pinch of salt. Give it a little whisk to combine.

In a jug, stir the puréed raspberries, evaporated milk, melted butter and eggs together and pour them over the dry ingredients. Gently mix to combine everything and give the bottom of the bowl a good scrape to make sure there are no dry bits of flour.

To finish:

a handful of fresh raspberries

a handful of chocolate chips
    or chunks

1 tsp freeze-dried raspberries

Pour the batter into the lined loaf tin and bake on the middle shelf for 60 to 65 minutes. Test with a skewer after 55 minutes, and if it doesn't come out clean pop the loaf back in the oven for another five minutes, then test again (you may need to do this more than once).

Leave to cool for half an hour or so in the tin, then lift the loaf out using the baking paper and set it on a cooling rack to cool completely.

Make a loaf batch of the Basic Buttercream on page 233, then gently melt the dark chocolate in a heatproof bowl over a pan of just-simmering water and set aside to cool a little. Stir the cooled chocolate into the buttercream so it's uniformly mixed through. Using a piping bag with an open nozzle, pipe thick zigzags of buttercream over the top and dot over the fresh raspberries, chocolate chips and freeze-dried raspberries.

Millionaire Shortbreads

We love Millionaire Shortbread so much we've included five recipes! Whichever one we put on the cake counter, it's guaranteed to sell out before everything else. There's just something about the combination of chocolate, thick caramel and biscuit that works so well – we keep coming up with different combinations. For most of them, we use a shortbread base based on the same recipe that inspired our Salted Caramel Crumble Bar. If the idea of making your own caramel is a little scary, please don't worry; it's really simple. It takes a little patience and a lot of stirring, but it's definitely worth it.

HANDY HINTS

- Don't skip the cold plate test. It's the best way to know if your caramel is ready.

- The caramel needs to be warm when poured and the base needs to be completely cool.

- Once topped, chill the millionaire for 30 minutes to set. However, you don't want it to get too cold or it's difficult to cut (with the exception of the vegan version, which is softer).

- To cut, use a large deep-bladed knife. Heat the knife in a jug of hot water and then dry it off. The hot blade will melt through the chocolate, making it much easier to cut.

- All the millionaires will keep for up to three days if you keep them cool and covered. The vegan millionaire is best kept in the fridge.

Millionaire Caramel

The Millionaire Caramel is a bit of a labour of love. Our bakery manager, Rachel, is the queen of caramel, mostly because she is endlessly patient and doesn't get frustrated by all the stirring. She makes the most perfect caramel every time. That said, the joy of cutting a slice of Millionaire Shortbread with perfectly thick caramel is worth all the stirring, we promise. And it tastes fantastic.

- Be super careful when making caramel. Boiling sugar is incredibly hot! Don't be tempted to taste or touch it until it has cooled down.

- If at any point during the process your caramel spits at you, turn the heat down. A long-handled spatula is highly recommended!

a big, heavy-based pan
a long-handled, heatproof spatula
   or spoon

350g unsalted butter, cubed
2 x 397g tins condensed milk
150g soft dark brown sugar
150g soft light brown sugar
4 tbsp maple syrup
1 tsp vanilla extract
1½ tsp sea salt flakes

Put a small plate in the freezer.

Put the butter, condensed milk, dark and light brown sugars, maple syrup, vanilla extract and sea salt in the pan over a low heat to melt. Stir regularly to stop it catching. Once it's all melted and you can't see any lumps of solid butter, turn the heat up to medium and keep stirring all the time until the mixture comes to the boil.

First you'll see big bubbles breaking, and then you'll start to notice small bubbles under the entire surface of the caramel. Keep boiling: it will start to look frothy in patches. Keep going until it looks frothy all over, then it's time to test the caramel.

Take the pan off the heat and take your plate out of the freezer. Spoon a little caramel onto the plate and give it a few minutes to cool down. Once cool, give the caramel a push with your finger: if it stays in place after you've pushed it, it's ready.

If it's still a little runny, boil for another minute and retest, repeating until it's ready. Let the caramel stand for ten minutes before pouring over your millionaire base.

Vegan Millionaire Caramel

It took a bit of trial and error to come up with a plant-based caramel as rich and indulgent as our dairy version, but in the end we found condensed coconut milk gave the best result. You can't really taste coconut, but it gives the caramel a richness and lovely colour.

200g unsalted plant-based butter, cubed
2 x 320g tins sweetened condensed coconut milk
150g soft dark brown sugar
150g soft light brown sugar
2 tbsp maple syrup
1 tsp vanilla extract
1½ tsp sea salt flakes

Follow the method on page 151, but once the caramel starts to look frothy all over set a timer for five minutes and keep boiling, stirring all the time. Test it, and if it's not quite ready boil for another minute and test again. Repeat until it stays in place on the plate.

Marshmallow Millionaire

This recipe is for anyone with a sweet tooth. It's big, generous and a huge seller in the bakery, possibly even the best selling of all the millionaires we do. The marshmallows melt a little and magically rise to make a chewy layer on top of the caramel. The bigger the marshmallows, the better! It looks great when it's sliced, as you see flashes of pink and white in the caramel.

- The shortbread dough is made using cold butter, so it's easiest to make it in a stand mixer or food processor.

- The number of marshmallows will depend on how big your traybake tin is. Our tray takes five rows of eight (which equates to two or three bags) but don't worry if you don't have quite enough – just space them out evenly on the base.

- Don't use mini marshmallows as they will melt completely and disappear into the caramel.

MAKES 12 GENEROUS SLICES

32 x 21cm traybake tin, lined

175g cold unsalted butter, chopped
100g caster sugar
75g icing sugar
1 tsp vanilla extract
250g plain flour

Preheat the oven to 180°C (160°C fan).

First make the base. Weigh the butter, caster and icing sugars and vanilla into a large bowl and beat (on low if you're using a mixer) until everything comes together and looks lighter in colour.

Add the flour and mix again until you have what looks like breadcrumbs. It won't come together as a dough. Tip the mixture into your lined traybake tin and press it down into an even layer with your fingers or the back of a spoon. Bake on the middle shelf of the oven for 25 minutes until light golden brown all over and leave to cool.

cont.

For the filling:
1 batch of Millionaire Caramel
   (page 151)
approx. 40 standard-sized
   marshmallows (we use a mix
   of white and pink)

To finish:
400g milk chocolate, melted

While the base is cooling, make the caramel (see page 151) and let it sit for ten minutes.

Cover the base completely with rows of marshmallows – lining them up neatly is a weirdly satisfying job!

Pour the slightly cool caramel gently over the marshmallow-covered base, being careful to get caramel between all the marshmallows, then pop it into the fridge or leave in a cool place for a few hours to set. The marshmallows may float to the top, or flip over, but hold your nerve; they all settle and end up evenly spaced throughout the caramel.

When the caramel is completely cold, pour over the melted chocolate and smooth it out. Pop it in the fridge for 30 minutes or so to set before slicing (see the tips on page 148 on how to achieve the perfect slice).

Brownie Cookie Millionaire

Millionaire Shortbread is incredibly popular in the bakery, and so are the gluten-free Triple Chocolate Brownie Cookies on page 63. So it made sense to us to come up with a recipe that combined both. This millionaire has a softer base than our other ones, and it's less sweet and more rich and dark thanks to lots of good dark cocoa powder and the 70% dark chocolate we use in the topping.

MAKES 12 GENEROUS SLICES

32 x 21cm traybake tin, lined

For the base:
130g chocolate chips (we use
    a mix of milk and white,
    but it's up to you)
3 medium eggs
350g icing sugar
30g cornflour
95g good quality cocoa powder
1 tsp sea salt flakes

For the filling:
1 batch of Millionaire Caramel
    (page 151)

To finish:
200g dark chocolate
200g white chocolate

Preheat the oven to 180°C (160°C).

Weigh the chocolate chips into one small bowl and crack your eggs into another. Put the icing sugar, cornflour, cocoa and sea salt into a large bowl and gently mix to combine.

Pour in your eggs and mix (on low if you're using a mixer) until everything is incorporated. It should be a fairly thick batter. Scape down the sides and bottom of the bowl to make sure you've mixed in all the dry ingredients. Add the chocolate chips and mix them evenly through the batter.

Dot spoons of the batter evenly across the bottom of the traybake tin and then start spreading it out with a spatula until you have an even layer, making sure you get it right into the corners. It is a sticky dough so just ease it into place.

Bake for 25 minutes until the base feels firm to the touch and has a papery-looking crust on top. It will firm up more as it cools.

While the base is cooling, make the caramel (see page 151) and let it sit for ten minutes. Pour it over the base and put it in a cool place or in the fridge for a few hours to cool completely. Melt the dark and white chocolate together in a heatproof bowl, either in the microwave or over a pan of just-simmering water. Pour the melted chocolate over the cooled caramel and smooth it out, then pop it in the fridge for 30 minutes or so to set before you slice it.

Vegan Hazelnut Millionaire

V

We really wanted to put a plant-based millionaire on the menu and after we'd mastered dairy-free caramel, we came up with this recipe. It's definitely as good as any of our dairy millionaires.

- Because the butter is cold, it's much easier to make the shortbread dough in a stand mixer or food processor.

- To roast the hazelnuts, put them on a baking tray in the oven at 180°C (160°C fan) for five to seven minutes. You can replace them with pecans or walnuts, or leave them out.

MAKES 12 GENEROUS SLICES

32 x 21cm traybake tin, lined

For the base:
250g cold unsalted plant-based butter, chopped
100g soft light brown sugar
75g icing sugar
1 tsp vanilla extract
275g plain flour
50g hazelnuts, very finely chopped

For the filling:
1 batch of Vegan Millionaire Caramel (page 152)
100g whole, skinless hazelnuts, roasted

For the topping:
300g vegan dark chocolate
50g chopped hazelnuts (optional)
handful of coconut flakes (optional)

Preheat the oven to 180°C (160°C fan). First make the base. Weigh the butter, soft brown and icing sugars and vanilla into a large bowl and beat (on low if you're using a mixer) until everything comes together and looks lighter in colour.

Add the flour and the chopped hazelnuts and mix again until you have what looks like breadcrumbs. It won't come together as a dough. Tip the mixture into your lined traybake tin and press it down into an even layer with your fingers or the back of a spoon. Bake on the middle shelf of the oven for 25 minutes until light golden brown all over and leave to cool.

While the base is cooling, make the Vegan Millionaire Caramel (see page 152) and let it sit for ten minutes. Pour the slightly cooled caramel over the base and dot the roasted, whole hazelnuts evenly over the top. Pop it into the fridge for a few hours to set. Gently melt the chocolate in a small heatproof bowl, either in the microwave or over a pan of just-simmering water. Pour the chocolate over the caramel and smooth it out into an even layer, then if you like sprinkle with chopped hazelnuts and coconut flakes. Put the millionaire back in the fridge for 30 minutes or so to set before slicing (see the guide on page 148 on how to achieve the perfect slice).

Chocolate Chip Cookie Millionaire

This one takes its inspiration from the Giant Chocolate Chip Cookie recipe on page 121. Generous in size and proportions, it's really popular in the bakery; there's no scrimping on the base, the chocolate or the caramel! It's a special-occasion kind of treat and definitely not something you'd bake every day. All that said, feel free to halve the amount of caramel in the recipe below if you'd like your bake a little less on the indulgent side.

- If you'd like a simpler finish, don't make the separate cookies – just use all the cookie dough rubble to make a thicker base. It might need a little longer in the oven.

- Freeze the leftover egg whites to use for the Meringue Frosting on page 243.

MAKES 12 GENEROUS SLICES

32 x 21cm traybake tin, lined
a baking sheet, lined

For the base:
175g plain flour
175g strong bread flour
75g cornflour
1 tsp salt
½ tsp baking powder
5 medium egg yolks
75g milk chocolate chips or chunks
75g white chocolate chips or chunks

Preheat the oven to 180°C (160°C fan).

Weigh your plain flour, bread flour and cornflour into a bowl with the salt and baking powder and stir to combine. Put the egg yolks in a jug and weigh the chocolate chips or chunks into a small bowl.

Cream the butter with the sugar and vanilla in your mixing bowl until the mix lightens in colour and looks less craggy. This takes minutes with a stand or hand-held mixer, but it will take a little longer with a mixing bowl and a spoon.

150g unsalted butter, softened
220g soft light brown sugar
1 tsp vanilla extract

For the filling:
1 batch of Millionaire Caramel
    (page 151)

To finish:
400g milk chocolate, melted

Scrape your bowl down and give it another mix, then add the flours and the egg yolks at the same time. Mix (on low if you're using a mixer) until everything is combined, scraping the bowl down as you go. Lastly, add in the chocolate chips and mix again until they are mixed through. The mixture will look like rubble.

Take 300g of this cookie dough rubble and divide into thirds to make the cookies for the top of your millionaire. Squeeze each third into a ball, place them on the lined baking sheet and pop in the fridge to chill for a few minutes.

Tip the remaining rubble into the lined traybake tin and press it down to make an even base layer, making sure the corners are as thick as the middle. Put both the base and the cookies in the oven at the same time. Check the cookies after 20 minutes – they are ready when they are golden brown and the middles feel set and firm-ish to the touch. The base will probably take five minutes longer – it too will be golden brown and firm, but not hard in the middle. Leave them both to cool completely in the tins while you get on with the caramel (see page 151).

Let the caramel stand for ten minutes, then pour it over the cool cookie base. Leave to set for a couple of hours in a cool place or in the fridge.

Now you're ready to finish off. Pour the melted chocolate over the caramel and smooth it out. Break up the three cookies into big chunks and scatter them over the top: you want them to sink into the chocolate layer a little.

Put the whole thing in the fridge for 30 minutes or so to set.

Celeb
Bakes

These are the big guns! From pretty cupcakes to towering layer cakes, these bakes are glamorous and impressive, perfect for a big party and so much easier to make than they look.

If we had a signature bake, it would be layer cakes. I started baking them back in the early days of Bad Girl, and while they have come a long way since then, they are still a favourite and we absolutely love baking them.

They are always three layers, giving (we think) the perfect ratio of sponge to filling. And they are never just buttercream and sponge either: we like to add hidden surprises, like biscuit pieces, fresh fruit, caramel and curds.

If you're nervous about piping or icing cakes, do look at pages 192 to 198. With just a few simple techniques, icing a big cake really is a lot easier than it looks, and if you've never done a crumb coat before, it will change everything! You won't find any fondant, sprinkles or artificial colour here, just pretty cakes decorated not only to look good but to add flavour, texture and colour that match the cake itself.

We couldn't write a book without including a few cupcake recipes. Even after all this time, they're still a firm favourite with our customers. If you can't face tackling a layer cake, or you need cakes for a smaller celebration, cupcakes are perfect. They are simple to make but look so pretty and eye catching.

ration

Cupcakes

The beauty of cupcakes is that you can knock up the cakes themselves very easily, then ice and decorate them to create something very special and celebratory. We are very generous (as ever) with our buttercream – if you like less buttercream, feel free to reduce the quantity a little. Once you've mastered the method, you can play endlessly with different fillings and flavoured buttercreams. Have fun!

CORING AND FILLING

Most of our cupcakes have a hidden filling. It's very easy: you can either use an apple corer or a small knife to take out the centre of the cake. Go deep, but not to the bottom of the cake. Use a teaspoon to fill the hole with caramel, curd, Dark Chocolate Glaze or whatever you like.

ICING CUPCAKES

Our cupcakes are piped with a smooth dome or swirl of buttercream. All you need is a piping bag and a large (ours is 1.6cm) plain or open nozzle.

Equipment:
piping bag with 1.6cm plain/open nozzle

Ingredients:
12 cupcakes
1 cupcake batch of buttercream (page 233)

For a dome:
Hold the piping bag just above the centre of the cake and squeeze steadily, moving the nozzle up slowly as you do.

You can get a similar effect using a large (ours is 58mm) scissor-action ice cream scoop – just place a scoop on top of each cake.

For a swirl:
Starting in the centre of the cupcake, squeeze steadily and pipe a spiral, just like a beehive, reducing the diameter every time you go round so you end up with a cone shape.

HANDY HINTS

- We don't recommend you use smaller cases; the cakes won't be big enough to hold the filling and they tend to dry out really quickly. The 52 x 40mm muffin cases we use can be found in the supermarket.

- Using a scissor-action ice cream scoop to ice each cupcake is a great trick if you're new to icing. Try to use one roughly the same diameter as the cupcake.

- If you're not confident with piping, practise on a plate till you've nailed it! You can just scoop the buttercream back into a bowl.

- If your piped dome is a little off centre, pick up the cupcake and gently shake it into place.

- Don't throw away the bits of cupcakes you core out. These can be frozen until you have enough to make the Cake Truffles on page 271.

- Cupcakes are really only good the day they are made.

Summer Berry Cupcakes

These cakes are so pretty! While they look very impressive, they are incredibly easy to make. It's worth making the very simple compote on page 251 to fill them, but really good jam would work too.

- Make the Berry Compote first as it needs to be cool before you use it.

- Freeze any leftover evaporated milk and use it to make Evaporated Milk & Strawberry Loaf (page 146) another time.

MAKES 12

12-cup muffin tin
12 large (52 x 40mm) muffin cases

For the cake:
200g unsalted butter, softened
200g caster sugar (we use
    Vanilla Sugar, see page 17)
1 tsp vanilla extract
4 medium eggs
200g self-raising flour
2 tbsp evaporated milk

For the buttercream:
1 cupcake batch of Basic
    Buttercream (page 233)
250g white chocolate,
    melted and cooled slightly

To finish:
½ batch of Berry Compote
    (page 251) or 1/2 a jar
    of good quality jam
6 large strawberries, halved
    lengthways
12 raspberries
24 blueberries
4 tbsp jam (optional)

Preheat your oven to 180°C (160°C fan).

Weigh the butter and caster sugar into a big mixing bowl or stand mixer and add the vanilla extract. Crack the eggs into a jug and weigh the flour into another bowl.

Beat the butter, sugar and vanilla together using your spatula (or a mixer on low) until it looks lighter in colour and less dense and craggy. It won't go really fluffy, but you will see a difference after three or four minutes of mixing. Scrape down the bottom and sides of the bowl to make sure you've got everything mixed in.

Pour an egg into the bowl and add a couple of spoons of flour, then beat until combined. Repeat with each egg, scraping the sides and bottom of the bowl between each addition. Gently mix in the remaining flour until it's all incorporated and stir in the evaporated milk.

Divide the batter equally between your cupcake cases (an ice cream scoop works wonders here) and bake for 20 to 25 minutes, testing with a skewer after 20. If the skewer comes out clean, they're ready. If not, pop them back in for two more minutes and test again, repeating until they are done. Do test each cake as bake times vary depending on where they are in the oven and how much batter is in each case. The tops should be golden brown. Leave the cakes to cool in their tins for 15 minutes before taking them out to let them cool completely on a cooling rack.

cont.

Make your Basic Buttercream on page 233 and mix in the cooled melted white chocolate. Using a piping bag with an open nozzle, pipe a dome of buttercream on each cake. If you don't have a piping bag you can use an ice cream scoop instead: take a flattened scoop of buttercream and place it on the cupcake, smoothing any ridges with a palette knife.

Put the brown sugar in a wide, shallow bowl. Take each cupcake, turn it upside down and press it gently into the brown sugar so you have an even layer over the top, brushing any clumps gently off with your fingers. Don't worry about flattening your dome of buttercream; that's exactly what you're after! You just want the sugar on the top, not the sides, as you don't want to torch the cupcake case. Pop the cupcakes in the fridge until the buttercream is hard to the touch.

Clear a big space and carefully blowtorch the top of each cupcake until the sugar melts to form a golden crust.

Chocolate Salted Caramel Cupcakes

These have been on our menu since the very beginning and I can't imagine the book without them. The recipe is very simple: the same chocolate cake used in the Triple Chocolate Cupcakes on page 180, filled with home-made caramel and topped with caramel buttercream and a sprinkle of sea salt. Even if you're not keen on the idea of salt on your cupcake, do give it a wee try; it seems to enhance the chocolate flavour and balance the sweetness of the caramel.

- If you're using our Soft Caramel, make it in advance so it has a chance to cool. You can use shop-bought instead; just add a little salt to taste.

- The flavour in the cakes comes from the cocoa powder, so do use the best, darkest brand you can find.

MAKES 12

12-cup muffin tray
12 large (52 x 40mm) muffin cases

225g self-raising flour
50g good quality cocoa powder,
   the darker the better
125g caster sugar
125g soft light brown sugar
100g unsalted butter, melted
25ml strong black coffee
200ml evaporated milk
1 medium egg
salt

Preheat the oven to 180°C (160°C fan).

Weigh out the flour, cocoa and the caster and light brown sugars into a big bowl or stand mixer with a pinch of salt and give it a quick mix to combine.

Whisk the melted butter, coffee, evaporated milk and egg together, then pour it over the dry ingredients and mix gently until everything is combined. Divide the batter between the cupcake cases using either a large ice cream scoop or a spoon.

Bake on the middle shelf of your oven for around 20 to 25 minutes, checking after 20 with a skewer. The cupcakes are ready when the skewer comes out clean and dry and the top feels springy to the touch. Every oven is different, so you may need to pop them back in for a few minutes and test again. Leave to cool in the tins for ten minutes, then transfer to a cooling rack to cool completely.

cont.

To finish:
½ batch of Soft Caramel
(page 244) or ½ tin
of shop-bought caramel
1 cupcake batch of Basic
Buttercream (page 233)
sea salt flakes (to taste)

Core out a hole in the centre of each cupcake using either an apple corer or a small knife and fill the holes with caramel.

Make the Basic Buttercream on page 233 and stir in two or three tablespoons of caramel. Using the piping bag with the open nozzle, pipe a dome of buttercream on each cake. If you don't have a piping bag you can use an ice cream scoop instead: take a flattened scoop of buttercream and place it on the cupcake, smoothing any ridges with a palette knife.

Drizzle the tops with a bit more caramel – if it's thickened too much, warm it just a little and give it a stir. Sprinkle a tiny pinch of sea salt flakes over each cake.

Vegan Chocolate Cupcakes

This recipe was a bit of a happy accident. I wanted to come up with a luscious, deeply chocolatey plant-based cupcake that would work well for a celebration. I love baking blogs and had seen a lot of American recipes that use mayonnaise in their chocolate cakes – not as surprising as it first sounds given that mayo is just oil and eggs. Granted, these recipes weren't vegan, but we use a lot of vegan mayo in our savoury kitchen so I thought I'd give it a try here. We're delighted with how it turned out and hope you like it too.

- If you like, you can fill the cupcakes with some strawberry jam

MAKES 12

12-cup muffin tin
12 large (52 x 40mm) muffin cases

175g self-raising flour
50g ground almonds
50g good quality cocoa powder,
   the darker the better
125g caster sugar
125 soft light brown sugar
1 tsp baking powder
200ml soya milk (almond milk
   works well here too)
100ml sunflower oil
25ml fresh coffee
1 tbsp vegan mayo
salt

Heat the oven to 180°C (160°C fan).

Weigh out the flour, ground almonds, cocoa, caster and light brown sugars and baking powder into a big bowl or stand mixer with a pinch of salt. Give it a quick mix to combine.

Measure the soya milk into a jug and add the oil, coffee and mayo. Whisk to combine, and don't worry if it looks curdled. Pour it over the dry ingredients and mix gently until everything is combined, scraping down the sides and bottom of the bowl so you catch any dry pockets of flour.

With a large ice cream scoop or a spoon, divide the batter equally between the cupcake cases in the tins. Bake on the middle shelf of your oven for around 20 to 25 minutes, checking with a skewer after 20. They are ready when the skewer comes out clean and dry and the top feels springy to the touch. Every oven is different, so you may need to pop them back in for a few minutes and test again. Leave the cupcakes to cool in the tins for ten minutes, then transfer to a cooling rack to cool completely.

cont.

To finish (optional):
1 cupcake batch of Vegan
   Buttercream (page 233)
250g vegan dark chocolate,
   melted

To decorate (optional):
100g vegan dark chocolate,
   melted
12 strawberries

Make the Basic Vegan Buttercream on page 233 and stir in the melted chocolate. Using a piping bag with an open nozzle, pipe a dome of buttercream on each cake. If you don't have a piping bag you can use an ice cream scoop instead: take a flattened scoop of buttercream and place it on the cupcake, smoothing any ridges with a palette knife. If you want to decorate the cupcakes, half dip the strawberries in melted chocolate and press one on top of each cupcake.

Variations

CHOCOLATE ORANGE
Add the zest of an orange to the cake batter and top with Chocolate Orange Buttercream (page 238).

CHOCOLATE RASPBERRY
Core the cooled cupcakes and fill with raspberry jam. Top with Raspberry Buttercream (page 237).

CHOCOLATE ALMOND
Replace the soya milk in the cake batter with almond milk. Core the cooled cupcakes and fill with almond butter, then top with Chocolate Buttercream (page 238) and a couple of toasted almonds.

TRIPLE CHOCOLATE
Core the cooled cupcakes and fill with cooled vegan Dark Chocolate Glaze on page 246. You can either let it cool just a little so it's the consistency of double cream, or leave it until it's as thick as peanut butter. It's up to you!

Triple Chocolate Cupcakes

Dark, chocolatey cupcakes filled with dark chocolate glaze, topped with white chocolate buttercream, and then dipped in the chocolate glaze. If you like chocolate, this is the recipe for you! Each step of the recipe is simple, but the results are impressive. Turning the cupcakes upside down to dip them in the glaze is a little nerve-racking, but we promise it works.

MAKES 12

12-cup muffin tin
12 large (52 x 40mm) muffin cases

225g self-raising flour
50g good quality cocoa powder,
  the darker the better
125g caster sugar
125g soft light brown sugar
100g unsalted butter, melted
25ml strong black coffee
200ml evaporated milk
1 medium egg
salt

To finish:
1 cupcake batch of Basic
  Buttercream (page 233)
250g white chocolate,
  melted and cooled slightly
1 batch of Dark Chocolate Glaze
  (page 246)

Preheat the oven to 180°C (160°C fan).

Weigh out the flour, cocoa and the caster and light brown sugars into a big bowl or stand mixer with a pinch of salt and give it a quick mix to combine.

Whisk the melted butter, coffee, evaporated milk and egg together, then pour the wet over the dry ingredients and mix gently until everything is combined. Divide the batter between the cupcake cases using either a large ice cream scoop or a spoon.

Bake on the middle shelf of your oven for around 20 to 25 minutes, checking after 20 with a skewer. The cupcakes are ready when the skewer comes out clean and dry and the top feels springy to the touch. Every oven is different, so you may need to pop them back in for a few minutes and test again. Leave to cool in the tins for ten minutes, then transfer to a cooling rack to cool completely.

cont.

Make the Dark Chocolate Glaze on page 246 and leave it to sit and thicken a little while the cupcakes are cooling. Then core out a hole in the centre of each cake using either an apple corer or a small knife and pour in the glaze.

Make the Basic Buttercream on page 233 and stir in the melted, cooled white chocolate. Using a piping bag with an open nozzle, pipe a whirl of buttercream on each cake. If you don't have a piping bag you can use an ice cream scoop instead: take a flattened scoop of buttercream and place it on the cupcake, smoothing any ridges with a palette knife.

Pop the cakes in the fridge for ten minutes to harden the buttercream. Put the remaining dark chocolate glaze in a small deep bowl. Take each cupcake and turn it upside down, then carefully dip the top into the glaze so all the buttercream is covered. Allow the excess to drip off before putting it down. Leave to set before serving.

Caramelised White Chocolate & Maple Honeycomb Cupcakes

Our lovely bakery manager, Rachel, came up with the idea of chocolate honeycomb cupcakes and they have always been a great seller. When caramelised white chocolate became a thing, I was keen to pair its rich, nutty flavour with maple syrup and these are the happy result.

- Make the Caramelised White Chocolate (page 249) and the Maple Syrup Honeycomb (page 259) the day before you want to eat these.

MAKES 12

12-cup muffin tin
12 large (52 x 40mm) muffin cases

200g unsalted butter, softened
150g caster sugar (we use
   Vanilla Sugar, page 17)
50g soft light brown sugar
1 tsp vanilla extract
4 medium eggs
200g self-raising flour
2 tbsp evaporated milk
1 tbsp maple syrup
50g Caramelised White Chocolate,
   finely chopped (page 249)

Preheat your oven to 180°C (160°C fan).

Weigh the butter and caster and light brown sugars into a big mixing bowl or stand mixer and add the vanilla extract. Crack the eggs into a jug and weigh the flour into another bowl.

Beat the butter, sugars and vanilla together using your spatula (or a mixer on low) until it looks lighter in colour and less dense and craggy. It won't go really fluffy, but you will see a difference after a few minutes of mixing. Scrape down the bottom and sides of the bowl to make sure you've got everything mixed in.

Pour an egg into the mix and add a couple of spoons of flour, then mix until combined. Repeat with each egg, scraping the sides and bottom of the bowl between each addition. Gently mix in the remaining flour until it's all incorporated, and add in the evaporated milk, maple syrup and finely chopped Caramelised White Chocolate. Stir to combine.

cont.

To finish:

1 cupcake batch of Basic
  Buttercream (page 233)
½ batch Maple Syrup Honeycomb
  (page 259)
250g Caramelised White
  Chocolate (page 249)

Divide the batter equally between your cupcake cases (an ice cream scoop works wonders here) and bake for 20 to 25 minutes, testing with a skewer after 20. If the skewer comes out clean, they're ready. If not, pop them back in for two more minutes and test again, repeating until they are done. Do test each cake as bake times vary depending on where they are in the oven and how much batter is in each case. The tops should be golden brown. Leave the cakes to cool in their tins for 15 minutes before taking them out to let them cool completely on a cooling rack.

Now you can get on with making the buttercream (see page 233): the fresher and softer it is, the easier it is to pipe. Once it's ready, take 50g of the Maple Syrup Honeycomb and either blitz it in a processor or bash it in a sandwich bag until you have crumbs. Fold these into your buttercream. Using the piping bag with the open nozzle, pipe a dome of buttercream on each cake. If you don't have a piping bag you can use an ice cream scoop instead: take a flattened scoop of buttercream and place it on the cupcake, smoothing any ridges with a palette knife.

Break the remaining maple honeycomb into large, jagged shards. Melt the Caramelised White Chocolate and dip in the shards so they are half-covered. Put one shard, chocolate side down, on the top of each cupcake, pressing it into the buttercream a little so the melted chocolate pools around it.

Loch Ness Gin & Tonic Cupcakes

We met the lovely folk at Loch Ness Sprits at a food and drink fair where we really hit it off and came up with the idea of a gin and tonic cupcake. It won an award at the National Cupcake Championships that same year. We only ever use their gin in our cupcakes, but feel free to use the gin of your choice. Go easy and test the filling and buttercream before adding more: some are stronger tasting than others. I have to say, tasting gin buttercream to check the gin levels might sound like a perk of the job, but it's a little less fun at 6am!

MAKES 12

12-cup muffin tray
12 large (52 x 40mm) muffin cases

200g unsalted butter, softened
200g caster sugar (we use
   Vanilla Sugar, page 17)
zest of 2 limes
1 tsp vanilla extract
4 medium eggs
200g self-raising flour
3 tbsp tonic water

Put your oven on to heat at 180°C (160°C fan).

Weigh the butter, sugar and lime zest into a big mixing bowl or stand mixer and add the vanilla extract. Crack the eggs into a jug and weigh the flour into a separate bowl. Beat the butter, sugar and lime together (on low if you're using a mixer) until the mixture lightens in colour and looks less dense and craggy. Scrape down the bottom and sides of the bowl to make sure you've got all the butter mixed in. Pour one egg into the bowl along with a couple of spoonfuls of flour and mix until everything is fully incorporated. Repeat with each egg, scraping the sides and bottom of the bowl every time. Finally, add in the rest of the flour, then gently mix in the tonic water.

Divide the batter equally between the 12 cases using either an ice cream scoop or a spoon. Bake for 20 to 25 minutes until the tops are golden brown, testing with a skewer after 20. If the skewer comes out clean, they're ready.

If not, pop them back in the oven for two minutes and check again – test each cake as bake times will vary depending on where it is in the oven and how much batter is in each case. Leave the cakes to cool in their tins for 15 minutes before putting them on a wire rack to cool completely.

cont.

To fill:

1 batch of Lime Curd (page 258)
or a jar of shop-bought
(you might not use it all)

1–2 tbsp gin

To finish:

1 cupcake batch of Basic
Buttercream (page 233)

zest of 1 lime

1–2 tbsp gin

12 lime wedges (use the
zested limes)

Mix the Lime Curd and gin for the filling, starting with a tablespoon of gin. Taste and add more if you fancy. Take an apple corer or a small sharp knife and core out the centre of the cake: you want a deep hole but the base of the cake left intact. Generously fill each hole with the curd and gin mix – it will settle so fill it slightly over the top of the hole. Keep the leftover curd to drizzle over the cupcakes later. Once that's done, you can get on with making the Basic Buttercream on page 233. Add most of the lime zest and a tablespoon of gin and stir well, then add more lime or gin to taste.

Using a piping bag with an open nozzle, pipe a dome of buttercream on each cake. If you don't have a piping bag you can use an ice cream scoop instead: take a level scoop of buttercream and place it on the cupcake, flattening any ridges with a palette knife.

Take the leftover curd and gin mix and give it a good stir. If it looks too thick to drizzle, thin it down with a tablespoon of tonic water, then drizzle a little bit over each cupcake. Place a lime wedge on top, zested side in the buttercream, to squeeze over the cupcake before you eat it.

Layer Cakes

We're not going to lie, it takes a bit of work to make one
of our layer cakes: you've got cake, buttercream and filling
to make, and then the assembly can be a little daunting
in itself. Don't be put off though – none of them are
difficult and the end results are something you'll feel
very proud of.

HANDY HINTS

- If you have to bake the three layers on separate shelves, adjust the top shelf down if you can so the cake is not too close to the top. Swap the cakes over after 20 minutes so the one on the top shelf can finish baking on the middle shelf.

- Do make sure the cakes are completely cool before you ice them. Even a tiny bit of residual heat will melt the buttercream and you'll end up with a melty, sliding mess!

- Don't throw away the sliced-off domes of the cakes. Put them in the freezer in a Tupperware to make Cake Truffles (page 271) or Leftover Cake Tiffin (page 269) another time.

- Chilled cakes are easier to cut, so if your buttercream is a little soft, chill in the fridge for ten minutes or so before cutting.

- Use a long, non-serrated knife and don't saw backwards and forwards, just gently push the knife down and pull it out once you've cut right through.

- For clean lines, wipe the knife clean after every cut.

- These are generous and tall three-layer cakes which will serve 10 to 12 people cut into slices. If you cut them into fingers, wedding cake style, you'll get more like 25 to 30 servings. Make a cut right down the cake about 3cm in from the edge, then cut this slab into fingers. Make another cut parallel to the first, another 2cm in. Cut this slab into 2-3cm fingers and repeat.

- Most of the layers will keep for up to two days once iced if kept refrigerated and well covered. If the cake has fresh fruit or meringue frosting on it, it's best decorated just before eating and eaten on the day. You can make the cake the day before and ice the day you are going to eat it if you prefer.

Pipe a rim of buttercream all around the edge of your first cake. It doesn't have to be neat.

Pipe a zig zag of buttercream in the centre of the cake and flatten it out using a palette knife or the back of a spoon. Don't flatten the rim of buttercream. You'll see that there is not a lot of buttercream in the centre – this not only gives you space for fillings, but also if you use too much buttercream between the layers they're likely to slide.

If you don't have a piping bag, dollop a blob of icing in the centre of the cake and smooth it out so it's about 5mm thick in the middle and about 10mm thick around the edge.

Next add your fillings. Again, be frugal (and we don't say that often) because overfilling can cause your layers to slide off. You're repeating the filling on the next layer so there will be plenty in your cake.

Take the second cake and place it cut side down on the layer you've just finished. Repeat the buttercream and filling as above. Place the final layer cut side down and look at your cake to see if it's even. If it looks a little wonky you can gently apply some pressure to the higher areas to even things up. There is a little give (remember the buttercream border).

Now you're ready to crumb coat. A crumb coat is a thin layer of buttercream over the whole cake to capture any crumbs, cover any imperfections and create a smooth surface onto which you will apply your final layer of buttercream. The key here is to go easy, applying small amounts of buttercream to the cake at a time, as any excess will be full of crumbs and you'll be unable to use it in your final layer.

Taking a spoonful at a time, use your long palette knife to spread buttercream all over the cake in an even layer. Remember, a little goes a long way! The aim is to capture all the crumbs; you should still be able to see the cake underneath. There's no real technique to this stage – just make sure that all the cake is covered.

Once the crumb coat is applied, pop the cake in the fridge or freezer to harden for 15 minutes, until the buttercream is firm to the touch, like cold butter. While it's chilling, pop the kettle on and clean down your surface. You don't want loose crumbs to end up on your cake.

Fill your tall jug with boiling water and set aside. You'll need your cloth too.

Get your cold cake and dollop lots of buttercream (the more the better) on the top. Using your palette knife, spread the buttercream all over your cake in a very thick layer. It will look really messy at this stage.

When the cake is completely covered and there are no bald spots, you can start to smooth it out. Holding your palette knife vertically and using big sweeping movements, smooth off the buttercream and pop any excess back in your bowl. If you need to, add more buttercream to cover the balder spots.

When all the excess is off and you have an even layer all the way round, it's time to start smoothing out to give you a clean, smooth surface all over your cake.

Wipe your palette knife clean, dip it into the jug of hot water for a few seconds, then dry it off with the clean cloth. With the flat of the knife against the side of the cake, smooth the surface of the buttercream using long movements.

Don't fret if you have a few lines on your cake. It doesn't need to be perfect! Also, once it's decorated no one will be looking at little imperfections on the sides.

Now decorate the top of your cake. You can use the remaining buttercream to pipe wee domes or whirls (see page 169 for piping techniques), scatter over edible decorations and drizzle with a glaze that complements the flavours in the cake. Take a wee look at some of our layer cakes in this chapter for inspiration.

Chocolate Caramel Fudge Layer

This incredibly chocolatey, rich and decadent layer is without a doubt our best-selling birthday cake. A quick glance at the ingredients will tell you it is a cake for a serious chocolate cake lover and definitely one to make for special occasions only! For all its grandeur (and it is pretty grand), it's really easy to make. We use our own caramel but a tin of the shop-bought stuff tastes just as good and you can skip it completely if you just fancy chocolate cake.

SERVES 10-12 (OR 25-30 WEDDING CAKE STYLE)

3 x 20cm sandwich tins, greased, then lined on the bottom only

480g self-raising flour
120g good quality cocoa powder, the darker the better
300g caster sugar
300g soft light brown sugar
¼ tsp salt
200g unsalted butter, melted
100ml strong black coffee
300ml evaporated milk
4 medium eggs
a pinch of salt

To finish:
1 layer cake batch of Basic Buttercream (page 233)
500g dark chocolate, melted and slightly cooled
1 batch Soft Caramel (page 244) or 1 x 397g tin of shop-bought

Preheat the oven to 180°C (160°C fan).

Place the flour, cocoa, caster and light brown sugars and salt into a big bowl and give it a quick mix to combine (on low if you're using a mixer).

Whisk the melted butter, coffee, evaporated milk and eggs together, then pour the wet over the dry ingredients. Mix gently until completely combined, scraping down the sides and bottom of the bowl to make sure you've caught any pockets of flour.

Divide the batter between the three greased and lined tins, smoothing it out using a palette knife or the back of a spoon. Bake for around 30 to 35 minutes. Check with a skewer after 30 – the cakes are ready when the skewer comes out clean and dry and the top feels springy to the touch. If not, pop them back in the oven for a few minutes and test again. Leave the cakes to cool in the tins for 30 minutes, then take them out and transfer to a cooling rack to cool completely. Make the Basic Buttercream on page 233 and stir in the cooled melted chocolate until fully combined. Once the cakes are completely cool, you can get on with assembling the cake. Ice it following the guide on page 195, filling each layer with two tablespoons of caramel. Once you've crumb coated and iced the top and sides, pipe dots of buttercream and caramel all round the top. Save any leftover caramel to drizzle over the cake when you serve it.

Choc Chip Cookie Layer

This cake is a monster! It's tall, impressive looking and tastes great, the kind of cake my thirteen-year-old son Felix would love for his birthday. The good news is that, although there are a few steps, this is really easy to make and you need little or no icing skills to make it look fantastic! If you're new at icing layer cakes, this one is a great place to start as the biscuit chunks in the buttercream hide a multitude of sins.

- If you're using shop-bought chocolate chip cookies, you'll need two or three in the buttercream and five or six to decorate the top.

- This will keep for up to two days once iced. Store the covered cake in the fridge and allow it to get to room temp before eating or the buttercream will be rock hard! You can make the cake the day before and ice the day you are going to eat it if you prefer.

SERVES 10-12 (OR 25-30 WEDDING CAKE STYLE)

3 x 20cm sandwich tins, greased, then lined on the bottom only

375g unsalted butter, softened
375g soft light brown sugar
2 tsp vanilla extract
6 medium eggs
375g self-raising flour

To finish:
1 layer cake batch of Basic Buttercream (page 233)
3 Giant Chocolate Chip Cookies (page 121) or 7–9 shop-bought chocolate chip cookies
150g milk chocolate, chips or chunks
2–3 tbsp caramel to drizzle (optional)
sea salt

Preheat your oven to 180°C (160°C fan).

Weigh the butter and light brown sugar into a big mixing bowl or stand mixer and add the vanilla extract. Crack the eggs into a jug and weigh the flour into another bowl.

Beat the butter, sugar and vanilla together using your spatula (or a mixer on low) until it looks lighter in colour and less dense and craggy. It won't go really fluffy, but you will see a difference after a few minutes of mixing. Scrape down the bottom and sides of the bowl to make sure you've got everything mixed in.

Pour an egg into the mix and add a couple of spoons of flour, then mix until combined. Repeat with each egg, scraping the sides and bottom of the bowl between each addition. Gently mix in the remaining flour until it's all incorporated. Divide the batter between the three tins and smooth it out using a palette knife or the back of a spoon. Place two tins on the middle shelf and one on the top shelf (or if you have a big oven put all the tins on the middle shelf so they bake evenly). Keep an eye on the one on the top shelf as it may bake quicker.

cont.

Spread three tablespoons of almond butter in the centre of the cake. Place the next layer on top, cut side down, and repeat with the remaining buttercream and almond butter. Then top with your final layer, again cut side down. See page 194 for more detailed instructions.

Apply a thin crumb coat of buttercream all over and put in the fridge for 15 minutes or until the buttercream is hard to the touch before finishing with a thick, perfect layer of icing on the top and sides. Sprinkle the toasted almonds round the edge.

To finish:

1 naked cake batch of Basic
  Buttercream (page 233)
zest of 1 lemon
1–2 tbsp elderflower cordial
6 tbsp Lemon Curd (page 257
  or shop-bought)
100g (approx.) fresh blueberries

To decorate (optional):
50g (approx.) fresh blueberries
few drops of lemon curd
lemon zest

Divide the batter between the three tins and smooth the mixture out using a palette knife or the back of a spoon. Dot blueberries over the tops of each cake.

Place two tins on the middle shelf and one on the top shelf (if you have a big oven, put all the tins on the middle shelf so they bake evenly). Keep an eye on the one on the top shelf as it may bake quicker. Bake for 25 to 30 minutes, testing with a skewer after 25. If the skewer comes out clean, the cakes are ready. If not, pop them back in for another five minutes and test again.

Leave the cakes to cool in their tins for half an hour before carefully running a palette knife round their outside edge and taking them out of the tin. Leave to cool completely on a cooling rack while you get on with making the Basic Buttercream on page 233. Flavour it with the lemon zest and a tablespoon of elderflower cordial, then taste and add more if you fancy. Now you can assemble and ice the cake following the guide on page 194. It's a naked cake so you just need to fill each layer with buttercream and three tablespoons of lemon curd and about 50g fresh blueberries, then pipe a layer of buttercream on the top.

Decorate with more fresh blueberries, dots of lemon curd and a scattering of lemon zest.

Lime Meringue Pie Layer

This cake is a beautiful showstopper. Layers of brown sugar lime sponge filled with buttercream, lime curd and biscuit chunks, and covered in toasted meringue. We're not going to lie; it's a lot of work, but none of the stages are difficult and you can make it over a couple of days. The results are worth it! Shop-bought biscuits and curd work really well here, so there's no need to make your own.

- You need a thermometer to make the Meringue Frosting.

- It's best to make the Meringue Frosting shortly before you are going to eat it as it doesn't keep. However, you can bake the cake the day before and fill and cover it the next.

SERVES 10-12 (OR 25-30 WEDDING CAKE STYLE)

3 x 20cm sandwich tins, greased, then lined on the bottom only
thermometer
kitchen blowtorch

375g unsalted butter, well softened
375g soft light brown sugar
2 tsp vanilla extract
zest of 2 limes
6 medium eggs
375g self-raising flour

Preheat the oven to 180°C (160°C fan).

Weigh the butter and light brown sugar into a big mixing bowl or stand mixer and add the vanilla extract and lime zest. Crack the eggs into a jug and weigh the flour into another bowl.

Beat the butter, sugar, vanilla and lime zest together using your spatula (or a mixer on low) until it looks lighter in colour and less dense and craggy. It won't go really fluffy, but you will see a difference after a few minutes. Scrape down the bottom and sides of the bowl to make sure you've got everything mixed in.

Pour an egg into the mix and add a couple of spoons of flour, then mix until combined. Repeat with each egg, scraping the sides and bottom of the bowl between each addition. Gently mix in the remaining flour until it's fully incorporated.

cont.

To finish:

1 loaf batch of Basic Buttercream
(page 233)

zest and juice of 1 lime

6 tbsp Lime Curd
(page 258 or shop-bought)

6–7 digestive biscuits, broken
into chunks

1 batch of Meringue Frosting
(page 243)

Divide the batter between the three tins and smooth it out using a palette knife or the back of a spoon. Place two tins on the middle shelf and one on the top shelf (if you have a big oven, put all the tins on the middle shelf so they bake evenly). Keep an eye on the one on the top shelf as it may bake quicker. Bake for 25 to 30 minutes, testing with a skewer after 25. If the skewer comes out clean, the cakes are ready. If not, pop them back in for another five minutes and test again. Do test each cake as bake times will vary depending on where it is in the oven and how much mix is in the tin.

Leave the cakes to cool in their tins for half an hour before running a palette knife round their outside edge and taking them out of the tin. Leave to cool completely on a cooling rack while you get on with making the Basic Buttercream on page 233. Stir the lime juice and zest into the finished buttercream.

Now you can fill and assemble the cake. Slice any domed tops off all the cakes and put one layer, cut side up, on your cake board, plate or turntable. Using either a piping bag or spatula, spread over half of the buttercream so it's about 5mm thick in the middle and about 10mm at the edge. Fill with three tablespoons of curd and three crumbled digestives. Place the next layer on top, cut side down, and repeat with the remaining buttercream, curd and digestives. Top with your final layer, again cut side down, and leave the top and the sides bare.

Shortly before you're going to eat the cake, make the Meringue Frosting on page 243 and cover the cake with it using a palette knife: you're going for a rustic, swirled look. Use the blowtorch to toast the frosting on the top and sides, and scatter over some biscuit crumbs if you fancy.

Boozy Chocolate Cherry Layer

This cake has been on our menu since the very beginning. The combination of dark chocolate and cherries is always a winner and it looks just beautiful. It's a great cake to start with if you're nervous about icing cakes, as the decoration is simple but super effective: it's a naked cake (meaning you just fill the layers and top with buttercream) and the only decoration is chocolate-dipped cherries. Maximum effect with just a little effort!

· You'll find jars of black cherries in kirsch in the baking aisle of the supermarket. Strain them through a colander into a bowl before you start. You need 125ml of the syrup to make the cakes, and then you'll use the cherries between the layers.

· If you'd rather make a non-boozy cake, replace the kirsch syrup with the same amount of coffee and double the amount of cherry jam to fill the cake.

SERVES 10-12 (OR 25-30 WEDDING CAKE STYLE)

3 x 20cm sandwich tins, greased, then lined on the bottom only

480g self-raising flour
120g good quality cocoa powder, the darker the better
300g caster sugar
300g soft light brown sugar
¼ tsp salt
200g unsalted butter, melted
125ml syrup from a 390g jar black cherries in kirsch
300ml evaporated milk
4 medium eggs

Preheat the oven to 180°C (160°C fan).

Place the flour, cocoa, caster and light brown sugars and salt into a big bowl and give it a quick mix to combine (on low if you're using a mixer).

Whisk the melted butter, kirsch syrup, evaporated milk and eggs together, then pour over the dry ingredients. Mix gently until completely combined, scraping down the sides and bottom of the bowl to make sure you've caught any pockets of flour.

Divide the batter between the three greased and lined tins, smoothing it out using a palette knife or the back of a spoon. Bake on the middle shelf of your oven for around 35 to 40 minutes. Check with a skewer after 30 – the cakes are ready when the skewer comes out clean and dry and the top feels springy to the touch. If not, pop them back in the oven for a few minutes and test again.

cont.

To finish:
1 naked cake batch of Basic
   Buttercream (page 233)
350g dark chocolate, melted and
   slightly cooled
6 tbsp cherry jam
cherries from a 390g jar of black
   cherries in kirsch

To decorate:
12 fresh cherries (with stalks on)
100g dark chocolate, melted
a few chocolate chips

Leave the cakes to cool in the tins for 30 minutes, then take them out and transfer to a cooling rack to cool completely.

Make the Basic Buttercream on page 233 and stir in the cooled melted chocolate. Once the cakes are completely cooled, you can get on with assembling and icing the cake following the guide on page 194. It's a naked cake, so use about a third of the buttercream for each layer and a third for the top. Fill each layer with three tablespoons of cherry jam and half of the reserved cherries from the jar.

For the decoration, half dip each of the fresh cherries in the final 100g of melted chocolate and leave to set on a sheet of greaseproof paper. Arrange them in a circle on the top of the cake and scatter over a few dark chocolate chips.

Sticky Toffee Layer with Browned Buttercream

Dark, sticky and rich, this cake is a favourite on our autumn menu. You might think cooking the dates in Coca-Cola is a little strange, but we wanted to get as much dark, molasses-like flavour in it as we could without making the sponge too heavy, and this seemed to work. You can replace the browned buttercream with caramel buttercream and the Brown Sugar Glaze with shop-bought caramel, but if you take the time to make it the way we do, we think you'll like it!

· You need to brown your butter for the buttercream (see page 240) the day before you make the cake.

SERVES 10-12 (OR 25-30 WEDDING CAKE STYLE)

3 x 20cm sandwich tins, greased, then lined on the bottom only

220g chopped, dried dates
200ml Coca-Cola (not diet)
250g unsalted butter, softened
260g soft light brown sugar
5 medium eggs
280g self-raising flour
1 tsp baking powder

To finish:
1 batch of Brown Sugar Glaze (page 248)
1 batch of Browned Buttercream (page 240)

Preheat the oven to 180°C (160°C fan).

Put the dates and the Coca-Cola in a small pan and simmer on a low heat until the liquid is almost all absorbed. Set aside to cool.

Weigh the butter and light brown sugar into a big mixing bowl or stand mixer. Crack the eggs into a jug and weigh the flour and baking powder into another bowl.

Beat the butter and sugar together using your spatula (or a mixer on low) until it looks lighter in colour and less dense and craggy. It won't go really fluffy, but you will see a difference after a few minutes of mixing. Scrape down the bottom and sides of the bowl to make sure you've got everything mixed in. Pour an egg into the bowl and add a couple of spoons of flour, then mix until combined. Repeat with each egg, scraping the sides and bottom of the bowl between each addition. Gently mix in the remaining flour, then mix in the cooled date mixture. Divide the batter between your lined tins, smoothing it out with a palette knife or the back of a spoon.

cont.

To finish:

1 batch of Brown Sugar Glaze
(page 248) or a 397g tin of
shop-bought caramel

1 layer cake batch of Basic
Buttercream (page 233)

2 tbsp espresso powder

12 pecan nuts, roasted (optional)

Pour an egg into the mix and add a couple of spoons of flour, then mix until combined. Repeat with each egg, scraping the sides and bottom of the bowl between each addition. Add in the remaining flour and the finely chopped roasted pecans and mix gently until it's all incorporated.

Divide the batter between the three tins and smooth it out using a palette knife or the back of a spoon. Place two tins on the middle shelf and one on the top shelf (if you have a big oven, put all the tins on the middle shelf so they bake evenly). Keep an eye on the one on the top shelf as it may bake quicker. Bake for 25 to 30 minutes, testing with a skewer after 25. If the skewer comes out clean, the cakes are ready. If not, pop them back in for another five minutes and test again. Do test each cake as bake times will vary depending on where it is in the oven and how much mix is in the tin.

Leave the cakes to cool in their tins for half an hour before running a palette knife round their outside edge and taking them out of the tin. Leave to cool completely on a cooling rack while you get on with making the Brown Sugar Glaze (page 248) and the Basic Buttercream (page 233). In a small bowl or cup, mix the espresso powder with a tablespoon of water, then beat this into the buttercream.

Now you can fill and assemble the cake following the guide on page 104. Fill each layer with a tablespoon of the cooled Brown Sugar Glaze – you only want a tiny hint of caramel here. Pop the fully iced cake in the fridge to harden the buttercream before you do the final decorations.

You need your Brown Sugar Glaze to be runny enough to drip down the sides of the cake – if it thickened up as it cooled, pop it in a heatproof bowl over a pan of hot water (off the heat) and give it a wee stir until it loosens up. You don't want any heat in the sauce as this will melt the buttercream. Spoon the sauce onto the cake and, using the back of a spoon, tease some over the sides so it drips down. Pop it back in the fridge for five minutes or so or until the caramel stops dripping. Once it's set, place the pecan nuts in a circle around the outside edge of the cake. If you skip setting the caramel up in the fridge, your pecans are likely to slide down the sides!

Raspberry Brownie Layer

This is dark, rich, dense (in a good way) and very, very chocolatey. The layers are based on our brownie recipe with a few wee tweaks, and the whole thing is super easy to make, especially if you go for the rustic finish in the picture. It's iced with chocolate glaze and you can change up the fillings and toppings to make any sort of chocolate combinations – we've given you a few ideas at the end of the recipe.

- Make a double batch of the Dark Chocolate Glaze on page 246 first, and leave it to cool as you bake the cake. You want it solid but spreadable, a bit like Nutella.

- The fresh fruit means this cake is best on the day it's made but leftovers can be enjoyed the next day if the cake is covered and stored in the fridge. Allow it to come to room temperature before you eat it.

SERVES 10–12, GENEROUSLY

3 x 20cm sandwich tins, greased, then lined on the bottom only

525g good 70% dark chocolate, chips or chopped
450g unsalted butter, cubed
300g caster sugar
300g soft light brown sugar
9 medium eggs
2½ tsp vanilla extract
225g self-raising flour
1½ tsp baking powder
1 shot of strong espresso (or 1 tbsp instant espresso dissolved in 1 tbsp of boiling water)
salt

Heat the oven to 180°C (160°C fan).

Weigh your chocolate and butter into a large heatproof bowl and melt them really slowly over a pan of just-simmering water. (We weigh ours directly into our stainless steel stand mixer bowl to minimise washing up.) Leave the melted chocolate to cool a little while you weigh out your other ingredients. Put the caster and light brown sugars into a bowl, then add in the eggs and the vanilla extract. Weigh the flour and baking powder into another small bowl and add a pinch of salt. Add the eggs and sugar mix to the cooled melted chocolate and mix with a spatula (or on low if you're using a mixer). Stir in the coffee, then fold in the flour until thoroughly combined. Give the bowl a good scrape with the spatula to make sure you've got it all.

cont.

To finish:
2 batches Dark Chocolate Glaze,
    cooled (page 246)
4–6 tbsp good quality
    raspberry jam
150g punnet of fresh raspberries
dark chocolate chips (optional)
freeze-dried raspberries (optional)

Divide the batter between the three tins and smooth the mixture out with the back of a spoon or a palette knife. Bake on the middle shelf for 25 to 30 minutes, checking with a skewer after 20. If there are one or two damp crumbs on the skewer, the cakes are ready. If there's any wet batter at all, they're underdone, so pop it back in the oven for five minutes and check again. Leave the cakes to cool in the tins for 30 minutes before carefully running a palette knife round the edge and removing them. Place them on a cooling rack to cool completely.

Take the first layer and place it on a cake board, or straight onto a cake stand or cake plate if you prefer. If it has baked with a dome in the middle, trim that off so you have a flat surface. Take two or three tablespoons from the cooled glaze and spread it all over the cake, allowing it to go over the sides. Spread two to three tablespoons of raspberry jam over the top, but not to the edges – leave a 2cm border all the way round.

Set aside ten raspberries for decorating the top, and arrange half of the remaining raspberries in a layer over the jam (again, not going to the edge of the cake). If the raspberries are huge, feel free to tear them in half to flatten them a bit. Repeat all of this with the second layer and then place the final layer on top with the bottom of the cake facing up (so you have a nice flat top on your cake).

Beat the remaining glaze with a whisk or mixer until it thickens and lightens in colour. Using a large palette knife, cover the cake generously with the whipped glaze and roughly smooth it out all over the cake. Any left over can be gently melted (over a pan of water or in the microwave) and served as a sauce with the finished cake.

Dot the ten fresh raspberries round the top, along with the chocolate chips and freeze-dried raspberries if you fancy.

Variations

CHERRY BROWNIE LAYER
Fill with cherry jam and fresh, stoned cherries (or drained cherries in kirsch) instead of raspberries.

ORANGE BROWNIE LAYER
Fill with orange curd and top with orange zest and chocolate chips.

Raspberry, White Chocolate & Rose Layer

This is such a pretty, natural, colourful cake, perfect for a summer birthday or party. The combination of sweet white chocolate and sharp raspberries is a winner, and the hint of rosewater makes it very special. It's also an easy cake to make and decorate and looks very impressive with very little effort! You can leave out the rosewater if you'd prefer: it will taste delicious either way.

- Because of the fresh fruit, this cake is best on the day it's made. You can make the cake the day before and ice the day you are going to eat it if you prefer. Leftovers can be refrigerated and eaten the next day.

SERVES 10-12 (OR 25-30 WEDDING CAKE STYLE)

3 x 20cm sandwich tins, greased, then lined on the bottom only

375g unsalted butter, softened
375g caster sugar
2 tsp vanilla extract
6 medium eggs
375g self-raising flour
100g white chocolate, finely chopped

To finish:
1 layer cake batch of Basic Buttercream (page 233)
1–2 drops rosewater

Preheat your oven to 180°C (160°C fan).

Weigh the butter and caster sugar into a big mixing bowl or stand mixer and add the vanilla extract. Crack the eggs into a jug and weigh the flour into another bowl.

Beat the butter, sugar and vanilla together using your spatula (or a mixer on low) until it looks lighter in colour and less dense and craggy. It won't go really fluffy, but you will see a difference after a few minutes of mixing. Scrape down the bottom and sides of the bowl to make sure you've got everything mixed in.

Pour an egg into the bowl and add a couple of spoons of flour, then mix until combined. Repeat with each egg, scraping the sides and bottom of the bowl between each addition. Add the remaining flour and the finely chopped white chocolate and mix gently until it's all incorporated.

cont.

100g fresh raspberries plus a few
  to decorate
4 tbsp good quality raspberry jam
rose Turkish delight, cut into small
  cubes (optional)
edible rose petals (optional)
white chocolate chips or chunks
  (optional)

Divide the batter between the three tins and smooth it out using a palette knife or the back of a spoon. Place two tins on the middle shelf and one on the top shelf (if you have a big oven, put all the tins on the middle shelf so they bake evenly). Keep an eye on the one on the top shelf as it may bake quicker. Bake for 25 to 30 minutes, testing with a skewer after 25. If the skewer comes out clean, the cakes are ready. If not, pop them back in for another five minutes and test again. Do test each cake as bake times will vary depending on where it is in the oven and how much mix is in the tin.

Leave the cakes to cool in their tins for half an hour before running a palette knife round their outside edge and taking them out of the tin. Leave to cool completely on a cooling rack while you get on with making the Basic Buttercream (page 233). Once it's done, stir in a drop of rosewater and taste – go easy as too much can taste soapy, but add another drop if you think it needs it. Add in three or four raspberries and mix thoroughly. If you'd like it more pink, add another three or four.

Now you can fill and assemble the cake following the guide on page 194. Fill each layer with two tablespoons of raspberry jam and half the remaining raspberries. Once it's fully iced, decorate the top with a circle of Turkish delight, rose petals and raspberries, and scatter with white chocolate chips. Gorgeous!

Buttercr
Fillings
Finishes

This chapter is all about finishing touches: everything from buttercream to custard and curds. While we use the recipes in the cakes and bakes in this book, they have loads of other uses too.

The Brown Sugar Glaze and the Dark Chocolate Glaze are great recipes to have up your sleeve. They are lovely as dips or over desserts and ice cream and are incredibly quick and simple to make.

The curds and compote are equally quick and simple and are definitely worth whipping up in their own right. The Custard Filling can also be used to fill cupcakes, layers and doughnuts or as a side to warm cakes, puddings and pies.

You'll also find lots of buttercream flavours here too, along with hints and tips on making perfectly smooth and delicious buttercream. With those under your belt you can mix and match them with the cake recipes to create your own layers, loaves and cupcakes.

ream, and s

DAY

ITEM _Caramel_ [R]
NAME _ß·cream_
QTY _____
DATE _30/4_
USE BY _____

VOGUE

Basic Buttercream

GF V

The truth is I was never really a fan of your average sickly-sweet buttercream. So we developed a method to make tasty, smooth, easy-to-work-with buttercream that works for cupcakes, loaves and layer cakes. This recipe is guaranteed to make piping cupcakes or icing layer cakes much, much easier – that's a promise! Douglas (Mr Bad Girl, who is not a baker) makes the very best buttercream every time, better than any of us bakers.

We've also included a version using plant-based butter. The method is exactly the same but there are a couple of tweaks to make it rich and smooth. Our head baker, Toni, absolutely loves vegan buttercream and prefers it to the dairy version. If you're a regular baker you'll notice this isn't a standard buttercream ratio, which is usually double the weight of icing sugar to butter. Ours has less sugar and it makes a soft, really tasty, smooth buttercream that isn't as sweet. Use this Basic Buttercream recipe – vegan or dairy – as a great base that you can flavour depending on what you're baking (see page 237 for some ideas for variations).

- Always use unsalted butter. You'd think salted would be ok, but it does make the buttercream salty.

- If you don't have a microwave, place your butter between two pieces of baking paper and bash it with a rolling pin till it's flat. Leave it on the counter for an hour or so and it should be soft enough.

- Our icing sugar comes in plastic bags and we use it so quickly that it never lumps, but if yours does please sieve it first. You'd think a few lumps would get knocked out when you're mixing the buttercream but they don't!

- Always use vanilla extract, not essence. It's more expensive but you need less and the taste is so much better.

- If you find that after adding the icing sugar your buttercream isn't soft enough, add a tablespoon or two of boiling water until it's soft and smooth.

- Any leftover plain buttercream will keep for three days in the fridge but will need to be softened and rewhipped before use.

DAIRY BUTTERCREAM

For a layer cake:
750g unsalted butter
2 tsp vanilla extract
1050g icing sugar

For a naked cake:
500g unsalted butter
1½ tsp vanilla extract
700g icing sugar

For a loaf or 23cm cake:
250g unsalted butter
1 tsp vanilla extract
350g icing sugar

For 12 cupcakes:
375g unsalted butter
1 tsp vanilla extract
525g icing sugar

VEGAN BUTTERCREAM

For a layer cake:
750g unsalted plant-based butter
2 tsp vanilla extract
1050g icing sugar
boiling water
salt

For a naked cake:
500g unsalted plant-based butter
1½ tsp vanilla extract
700g icing sugar
boiling water
salt

For a loaf or 23cm cake:
250g unsalted plant-based butter
1 tsp vanilla extract
350g icing sugar
boiling water
salt

For 12 cupcakes:
375g unsalted plant-based butter
1 tsp vanilla extract
525g icing sugar
boiling water
salt

You'll need a stand mixer with a paddle attachment or a hand-held mixer with the two attachments (not a stick blender). This is one of the few times when a bowl and elbow grease won't cut it, I'm afraid!

Put the butter on a plate and microwave on medium for one to two minutes, or until the butter is really, really soft. Check it every 30 seconds: you want to be able to put your finger straight through the middle of it. You should see just a little liquid butter on the plate too.

Tip the butter (including any that's completely melted) into the mixer bowl along with the vanilla and mix until completely smooth. Don't rush this stage; what you want is completely smooth butter with no lumps at all.

When it's completely smooth, add in the icing sugar. If you have a shield for your mixer, then you can add the whole lot at once. If not, you will need to keep the mixer really low and add it gradually. Once it's all incorporated, turn the speed up to medium and keep mixing until it's super smooth. It will go lighter in colour and texture. If you're making Vegan Buttercream, you'll now need to add boiling water, a tablespoon at a time, until it is soft and smooth. The amount you'll need will depend on the brand of butter you use.

And that's you! We always say it looks like Mr Whippy ice cream when it's ready.

The vegan version really needs a pinch of salt at this point – mix it in well and taste. The buttercream won't taste salty, but it should make it a little richer. Feel free to add a little bit more if you fancy.

Flavoured Buttercreams

Plain buttercream is a great base for lots of other flavours and textures: the following recipes are the ones we use on our layer cakes, topped loaves and cupcakes. The trick is to follow the recipe on page 233 so you have a lovely, smooth, soft buttercream before you add in the additional flavouring. We're not big on artificial colours and flavours so these additions are all natural.

- Buttercream doesn't like a lot of liquid, so go easy when adding coffee, lemon juice, raspberries, etc. Always give it a taste and add more of whatever you think it needs.

- Flavoured buttercream is best used as soon as it's made. We find it doesn't keep as well as plain vanilla buttercream.

Once you have made whatever quantity of Basic Buttercream, just leave it in the mixer and follow the directions below.

WHITE CHOCOLATE BUTTERCREAM

Layer cake:	500g white chocolate
Naked cake:	350g
Loaf/23cm cake:	150g
Cupcakes:	250g

Gently melt the white chocolate and set aside to cool for 15 minutes or so, then add it to the buttercream and mix.

RASPBERRY BUTTERCREAM

Add raspberries, two or three at a time, to the buttercream and mix. They will give the buttercream a lovely, natural pink colour and their tart flavour cuts the sweetness. Keep adding them until you get the colour and flavour you want, but go easy as it can turn neon pink very quickly!

LEMON BUTTERCREAM

Add the zest of half a lemon (or a whole lemon for a layer cake or naked cake) to your buttercream and mix well. Feel free to add more if you like a stronger flavour. The little flecks of yellow on your finished cake look so pretty! You can add a little lemon juice to intensify the flavour but go easy as too much can split the buttercream.

LIME BUTTERCREAM

As for Lemon Buttercream, but use lime zest. You may have to add the zest of another lime if the flavour isn't strong enough.

cont.

ORANGE BUTTERCREAM

As for Lemon Buttercream, but use orange zest. You may have to add the zest of another orange if the flavour isn't strong enough.

CARAMEL BUTTERCREAM

Layer cake:	3–4 tbsp Brown Sugar Glaze (page 248) or shop-bought caramel
Naked cake:	2–3 tbsp
Loaf/23cm cake:	1–2 tbsp
Cupcakes:	1–2 tbsp

Thoroughly mix in the glaze or caramel, then taste and add more if you think it needs it. Go easy as very caramelly buttercream doesn't set up firmly and can make icing a cake tricky.

SALTED CARAMEL BUTTERCREAM

As for Caramel Buttercream, but add a pinch of salt.

COFFEE BUTTERCREAM

Layer cake:	2 tbsp instant espresso powder
Naked cake:	1½ tbsp
Loaf/23cm cake:	1 tbsp
Cupcakes:	1 tbsp

Mix the espresso powder with a tablespoon of water, then add the paste to your buttercream and mix well. Taste and add more if you fancy.

DARK CHOCOLATE BUTTERCREAM

Layer cake:	500g 70% chocolate
Naked cake:	350g
Loaf/23cm cake:	150g
Cupcakes:	250g

Gently melt the chocolate and set aside to cool for 15 minutes. Add to the buttercream and mix thoroughly.

CHOCOLATE ORANGE BUTTERCREAM

As for Dark Chocolate Buttercream but add the zest of an orange.

CHOCOLATE MINT BUTTERCREAM

As for Dark Chocolate Buttercream but add a drop or two of peppermint extract, tasting after each drop. Go easy as it can pretty quickly taste a bit like toothpaste if you put too much in!

CHOCOLATE CHILLI BUTTERCREAM

As for Dark Chocolate Buttercream but add a couple of pinches of chilli flakes. Taste and add more if you fancy.

MOCHA BUTTERCREAM

As for Dark Chocolate Buttercream but mix two tablespoons of instant espresso powder mixed with a tablespoon of water. Taste and add more if you fancy.

CHOCOLATE CHIP COOKIE
BUTTERCREAM

Layer cake:	1 Giant Chocolate Chip Cookie (page 121) or 2–3 shop-bought cookies
Naked cake:	1 Giant Chocolate Chip Cookie or 1–2 shop-bought
Loaf/23cm cake:	½ Giant Chocolate Chip Cookie or 1–2 shop-bought
Cupcakes:	½ Giant Chocolate Chip Cookie or 1–2 shop-bought

Chop up the cookie and add it to your buttercream. Mix well – the mixing will break down any big chunks, but don't worry if there are still some. You want to be able to see that the buttercream has cookies in it.

HONEYCOMB BUTTERCREAM

Layer cake:	3 or 4 shards of honeycomb (page 259)
Naked cake:	3 or 4 shards
Loaf/23cm:	2 shards
Cupcakes:	2 shards

Whizz up the honeycomb in a processor. Add to your buttercream and mix well.

Browned Buttercream GF

This is the buttercream we use to ice our Sticky Toffee Layer on page 219. Browning the butter first makes it taste sweet and nutty and much deeper in flavour. It's the perfect buttercream for any autumnal cake: think sticky, dark, ginger, apple and date flavours. It takes a little time to make, but it's worth the effort. Be super careful as the butter can easily burn if you don't watch it like a hawk. Give yourself plenty of time to make this. It takes a while to brown the butter, as you're doing such a big quantity, and then you need to chill it before making the buttercream. We often brown it the day before we make the buttercream.

- Please be careful when browning the butter – it burns very easily. Take your time and don't take your eyes off it.

- If you're using shop-bought caramel, give it a taste after you've added two tablespoons. It's much sweeter than our Brown Sugar Glaze so you might need to add a pinch of salt.

MAKES 1 LAYER CAKE BATCH

A stand mixer with a paddle attachment or a hand-held mixer with the two whisk-like attachments (not a stick blender).

750g unsalted butter, cubed
1 tsp vanilla extract
700g icing sugar
4–6 tbsp Brown Sugar Glaze
    (page 248) or shop-bought
    caramel

First you need to brown the butter. Put the cubed butter in a big, deep, sturdy pan on a low heat until it melts, then turn up the heat to medium-low. The milk solids will gather in a layer on top, then as it gets hotter they will sink into the melted butter and start to brown. Once the foam has subsided, the butter will slowly deepen in colour until it is flecked with little bits of brown – the smell is rich and nutty. Whatever you do, don't take your eye off the pan and stir frequently. It takes a little time, patience and stirring, but please don't be tempted to turn up the heat to speed things up. This process should be gentle and slow. It can take up to 20 minutes.

Set the pan aside and let the butter cool for half an hour or so, then pour it into a heatproof bowl, cover and pop in the fridge to harden. We tend to do this the day before we need it.

Once it's solid, you can go ahead and make the buttercream. Soften the butter a little in the microwave, then scrape it into your mixer bowl and add the vanilla. Beat them together until smooth and then slowly add the icing sugar. Mix on medium until everything is combined: it will look a bit dry and grainy.

Add four heaped tablespoons of cooled Brown Sugar Glaze and mix. Taste the buttercream and add a tablespoon or two more glaze if you think it needs it. If the buttercream is still a little stiff, beat in one or two tablespoons of boiling water and mix. You can add a bit more if you need too: it just needs to be soft and whipped-looking. It's now ready to use.

Soft Caramel

This is the soft caramel we use in our Salted Caramel Crumble Bar, brownie and layer cakes: basically the same recipe as our Millionaire Caramel, just boiled for less time. It tastes wonderful and keeps for three days in the fridge, so it's a very useful ingredient to have on hand.

- Be super careful when making caramel. Boiling sugar is incredibly hot! Don't be tempted to taste or touch it until it's cooled down.

- Store the caramel in a Tupperware in the fridge and stir a little to loosen it before you use it, or heat it gently in the microwave or in a pan.

a big, heavy-based pan
a long-handled heatproof
   spatula or spoon

175g unsalted butter, cubed
1 x 397g tin condensed milk
75g soft dark brown sugar
75g soft light brown sugar
2 tbsp maple syrup
½ tsp vanilla extract
½ tsp sea salt flakes

Put the butter, condensed milk, dark and light brown sugars, maple syrup, vanilla and sea salt in a big, heavy-based pan. Put over a low heat to melt. Stir regularly to stop it catching. Once it's all melted and you can't see any lumps of solid butter, turn the heat up to medium and keep stirring all the time until the mixture comes to the boil.

Once the mixture is boiling and there are big bubbles breaking all over the surface, take it off the heat. Leave the caramel to cool before using.

Dark Chocolate Glaze <u>GF</u> <u>V</u>

This rich, dark glaze is very versatile. We use it to top our Triple Chocolate Cupcakes (page 180), as a sauce in our Caramel Brownie Sundaes (page 272) and, once cool, whipped up as the icing on our Raspberry Brownie Layer Cake (page 225). It's lovely poured over ice cream, or you can serve a little ramekin with strawberries, biscuits or meringue pieces to dip in it. It's also super easy to make a vegan version, which can be used in exactly the same way: just use plant-based butter and make sure your chocolate is vegan.

- Don't be tempted to whack the heat up. It really does work best if you take your time.

- Use good quality, 70% dark chocolate. It gives the glaze its rich, deep taste and dark colour.

- The pinch of salt makes all the difference: it won't taste salty, we promise!

- The glaze keeps for two to three days in a Tupperware in the fridge. It will solidify, but you can gently re-melt it in the microwave on low, or over a pan of just-simmering water.

MAKES ENOUGH TO GLAZE 12 CUPCAKES, AND WE DOUBLE IT TO ICE THE LAYER CAKE

200g really good 70% dark chocolate
120g unsalted butter or plant-based butter, chopped into small cubes
60g golden syrup
sea salt flakes

Put the chocolate, butter and syrup into a heatproof bowl and set it over a pan with a couple of inches of water in the bottom. Make sure your heatproof bowl is well above the water. Put the pan on a low heat and let the water come to a simmer (you can lift the bowl to check but watch out for the steam).

Things will start to melt really gently. Give it a stir from time to time and take the pan off the heat before everything is completely melted, when you can still see little lumps of almost-melted butter. The heat in the bowl will carry on melting everything and you won't run the risk of burning the chocolate. Stir in a pinch of salt once it's off the heat.

Brown Sugar Glaze

This is another great recipe to have up your sleeve. It's super simple and quick to make with a lovely treacly flavour and a beautiful shine to it. We use it to glaze and fill our Sticky Toffee Layer (page 219) and to top the Sticky Toffee Pecan Slice on page 137. You can of course drizzle it over ice cream, make sundaes with it and use it like a fondue too.

The quantity below makes enough for either of the cakes above, but you can multiply this up easily to make as much as you like.

- Don't be tempted to whack the heat up. You really don't want to heat this much at all.

- The pinch of salt makes all the difference to the glaze, without making it taste salty. Don't leave it out!

- The glaze thickens on cooling, so if you're using it as a filling or topping for a cake, let it cool to room temperature first. If you're using it as a dip or a sauce, it's ready straight away.

- This will keep for two to three days in the fridge. It doesn't solidify, but you might want to gently warm it through before using.

175g soft dark brown sugar
125g unsalted butter, chopped into
   small cubes
150ml evaporated milk
2 tsp vanilla extract
sea salt flakes

Measure the sugar, butter, evaporated milk and vanilla into a small saucepan and melt everything really gently over a low heat. You don't want too much heat in this: you just need to melt the butter and dissolve the sugar slowly, without even bringing it to a simmer. Take your time and stir every couple of minutes.

When everything is melted together, take it off the heat and stir in a pinch of salt. Take a teaspoon of the glaze and let it cool for a minute or two. Put a little on your index finger and rub your finger and thumb together: you shouldn't feel any graininess from the sugar. If it feels smooth, it's ready. If it still feels a little grainy, pop it back on the heat and test again after a minute.

Caramelised White Chocolate

Caramelising chocolate takes a little time and patience, but there is nothing complicated to it at all. It takes a fair bit of stirring but it's something you can do while you're doing other jobs in the kitchen, and it really is worth taking the time to do it. The flavour is difficult to describe: it tastes nutty and caramelly and reminds us all of Caramac bars.

One batch is enough for our Caramelised White Chocolate & Pecan Shortbread on page 69 or the Caramelised White Chocolate & Maple Honeycomb Cupcakes on page 185.

MAKES 300G

300g white chocolate

Preheat your oven to 140°C (120°C fan).

Put the white chocolate in a heatproof dish (we use an unlined baking tray) and pop it in the oven on the middle shelf. Every ten minutes (you'll need a timer), take it out and give it a really good stir with a spatula before popping it back in the oven. Do this for about an hour until the chocolate is smooth and golden brown (like a Caramac bar!). Don't worry if your chocolate looks lumpy at any point – that's normal. Just flatten out the lumps with your spatula and stir well. Scrape the chocolate into a small Tupperware container lined with baking paper (so you can pull the chocolate out using the paper later). You want it to harden into a nice thick layer so you can chop it into good-sized chunks. Set aside to cool completely and store in a cool place for up to three days.

Berry Compote

We use this all the time! It takes no time at all and has so many uses: we use it to fill layer cakes and cupcakes, and alongside French toast or toasted banana bread. It's delicious with yoghurt, ice cream and over porridge. It's a great way to use up leftover berries, but it's worth knowing that frozen berries make great compote, and there's no need to defrost them first.

- This will keep for up to three days in the fridge and freezes well.

- For vegan compote use maple syrup instead of honey.

- This tastes (and looks) better with a mix of berries, so frozen berries are a great choice. Most supermarkets sell bags of imperfect berries which are much cheaper and perfect for this recipe.

MAKES AROUND 450G OF COMPOTE

500g fresh or frozen berries
(no need to defrost)
100g sugar (we use Vanilla Sugar,
page 17)
2 tbsp honey
juice of half a lemon

Put the berries, sugar, honey and lemon juice in a pan on a medium-high heat, stirring frequently so the sugar doesn't burn. Let it boil for 10 to 15 minutes or so (though if your berries are fresh it may take less time).

When the juice starts to look syrupy and coats the back of the spoon, it's ready. It will thicken as it cools. If the compote is too watery it will make cakes soggy, so don't take it off the heat too early.

Allow the compote to cool completely before using.

Kathleen's Apple Jelly GF V

We get through a lot of apple jelly in the bakery and it's always my mother-in-law Kathleen's recipe. It's based on one from the *Edinburgh Book of Plain Cookery* which was given to Kathleen by her Auntie Belle for Christmas 1963, and she still makes it for us now. I remember getting my first jelly pan and making a batch of this from the windfall apples in the garden and feeling all sorts of proud and domesticated!

It's a really useful thing to have in your store cupboard. It makes a lovely glaze, enhancing flavours and giving cakes a pretty shine, but it's also delicious on toast or scones, or with burgers, pork or cheese.

The recipe works with any sort of apple at all, including windfalls and apples that are maybe starting to go a little wrinkly. We only use one kind of apple per batch so they cook at the same time. I love the way the recipe is written as it means you can make jelly with however many apples you've got. We've left the weights in pounds and pints in tribute to the original recipe.

- The smallest number of apples you can make this with is six. If so, reduce the jelly boiling time to around ten minutes but do the frozen plate test after eight.

- When you strain the apples, it looks like there's not a lot of liquid, but leave them to strain for half an hour or so and you'll get much more out of them. If you're using a lot of apples, you might have to strain them in batches.

- Different apples give different amounts of juice, so you might need different amounts of sugar every time.

- Do use a really big pot as you'll need lots of space for boiling. Be super careful when boiling the jelly as it's really, really hot!

- This will keep for up to three months unopened if stored somewhere cool, and for a week or so in the fridge once opened.

- The yield will vary depending on the sizes of your apples and how juicy they are, but we tend to get approximately one 300ml jar for every six small, red eating apples.

cont.

big pot or jelly pan
long-handled heatproof spoon
jelly bag or large muslin square
large heatproof bowl
sterilised jars, lids and wax circles

apples, washed and cut into
    quarters (don't peel or core
    them)
½lb granulated sugar plus ½lb jam
    sugar for every pint of juice

Put a saucer or a small plate in the freezer (you'll need this for testing the jelly later on).

Put your quartered apples in a big pot and just cover them (and no more) in cold water. Make sure your pan is no more than half filled as you'll need plenty of space for boiling safely.

Bring to the boil and continue boiling, uncovered, over a medium heat, until the apples have disintegrated into pulp (ours takes around an hour). Spoon the pulp into a jelly bag (or colander lined with muslin) hanging over a bowl and allow the juice to strain. Don't squeeze or push the pulp through or your juice will be cloudy.

While the apple pulp is straining, clean your pan ready to use again and sterilise your jars and lids.

Measure the juice to see how much you've got, then pour it back into the clean pan. For each pint of juice, add a pound of sugar – half granulated and half jam sugar. Stir over a low heat until all the sugar is dissolved and then bring to a boil for 15 minutes. Skim off any scum that gathers and discard it.

Take a teaspoon of the jelly and pop it on the frozen plate. If it's ready it will hold its shape. If not, boil for another three to five minutes and test again.

When it's ready, spoon the jelly into your sterilised jars. Top with a wax circle and put the lid on straight away.

Custard Filling

This thick, rich custard has so many uses. We fill our brioche tarts and breakfast pastries with it, you can use it to fill cakes and cupcakes and it's also really lovely served warm with pudding too. It's very easy to make, but don't be tempted to rush it or you'll taste the flour and the custard won't thicken. Our head baker, Toni, makes the best custard; she's endlessly patient and really enjoys all the whisking!

- Although best on the day, the custard will keep for up to two days in the fridge.

- You can lighten the cooled custard by mixing in some whipped cream.

25g cornflour
125ml evaporated milk
3 medium egg yolks
60g caster sugar
1 tsp vanilla extract
125ml double cream

Dissolve the cornflour in two or three tablespoons of the evaporated milk and set aside.

In a bowl, whisk the egg yolks, sugar and vanilla together and add the cornflour mixture. Put the rest of the evaporated milk and the cream in a small pan and gently bring to a boil. Pour it over the eggs, whisking non-stop until everything is combined.

Pour the mixture back into the pan and gently bring back to a boil. Cook for two to three minutes, whisking all the time, and then turn the heat down and continue cooking for another minute or two until the custard is thick and glossy and coats the back of a spoon. It will thicken a lot more as it cools.

Cover by putting cling film directly on the surface and chill before using.

Heather's Lemon Curd GF

This is the lemon curd my mum always makes. I don't know the origins of the recipe, and my mum can't remember where she found it, but she has been making it for years (mostly for my brother-in-law Niall, who loves it) and I'm delighted to include it here. We fill cupcakes and layer cakes with it, but it's also wonderful on toast and scones.

It's an easy recipe to play around with: we make a grapefruit variation for our Pink Grapefruit Meringue Shortbread Tarts on page 131. We used to buy our lime curd from a lovely local supplier, Struan Apiaries, but since they stopped producing it, we use the recipe below. My mum always makes hers in the microwave, but I've included a stove top method too. If you're making it on the stove, it needs constant whisking; in a microwave version, less so. Choose whichever suits you best – the results are the same.

- Don't be tempted to speed the process up and take the curd off too early. The eggs need to be fully cooked and the curd should be thick.

- You can strain the zest out using a sterilised sieve, but we leave ours in as we think it adds to the flavour.

- Curd keeps for up to two weeks in a sealed, sterilised jar in the fridge, and for a week or so in the fridge once opened.

MAKES APPROX. 500ML

2 sterilised jars with lids and wax circles

zest and juice of 6 lemons
75g unsalted butter, cubed
225g sugar
4 medium eggs, beaten

MICROWAVE METHOD

Put the lemon zest, juice and butter into your bowl and cook on full for three minutes until the butter has melted. Give this a stir, then add in the sugar and cook on full for two minutes.

Stir until the sugar is dissolved, then pour in the beaten eggs, stirring all the time. You need to stir the moment the eggs hit the butter mixture.

cont.

Pop it back in the microwave and cook on low for 15 minutes (it can take anywhere between 12 and 16 minutes depending on the microwave). Take it out every three or four minutes and stir. The curd is ready when it's thick enough to coat the back of a spoon. Be careful when taking the bowl out of the microwave as it will be very hot.

Spoon the curd into the sterilised jars and top with a wax circle. Allow to cool before putting the lids on.

STOVE TOP METHOD
Put the lemon zest, juice, butter and sugar into your bowl and place it over a pan of simmering water, making sure the water isn't touching the bowl. Stir until the butter has melted and the sugar has dissolved and then pour in the eggs, stirring all the time. You need to stir the moment the eggs hit the butter mixture.

Keep whisking all the time until the curd has thickened and is cooked – around 15 to 17 minutes. The curd is ready when it's thick enough to coat the back of a spoon.

Spoon the curd into the sterilised jars and top with a wax circle. Allow to cool before putting the lids on.

Variations

LIME CURD
Replace the lemons with limes and follow either method above. We strain the zest out of the curd as it gives it a much nicer colour and texture. You will get 1 x 320ml jar out of this.

GRAPEFRUIT CURD
Replace the lemons with the juice of one grapefruit and the zest of half – we always use pink grapefruit. This curd tends to take longer to cook – 20 minutes or so in the stove top method.

Maple Syrup Honeycomb

This was the inspiration behind our Caramelised White Chocolate & Maple Honeycomb Cupcakes on page 185. Sweet, salty and slightly smoky, it makes a dramatic topping on a cupcake or layer cake, and shards dipped in chocolate and left to set make a lovely gift. My son Felix likes it crumbled on ice cream too. It's not a difficult recipe but it's really important to get the sugar hot enough or it will collapse when it sets. If you have a sugar thermometer, now's the time to get it out!

- Use 100% pure maple syrup as that's what gives the honeycomb its flavour.

- It will keep for around a week in an airtight container. Don't put it in the fridge or anywhere damp.

long-handled heatproof
  spatula or spoon
traybake tin, lined with
  greaseproof paper
sugar thermometer or
  a bowl of cold water

200g caster sugar
3 tbsp golden syrup
2 tbsp maple syrup
2 tsp bicarbonate of soda

First thing to do is get all your ingredients ready and line your tin, as the last stage of the recipe has to be done quickly. If you don't have a sugar thermometer, set the bowl of cold water next to your hob.

Weigh the sugar, golden syrup and maple syrup directly into a medium-sized pan, then put it on a low heat to melt slowly. Swirl the pan around to help things along and give it the occasional stir if you need to. Be patient here as you don't want the mix to get too hot and bubble before the sugar has melted.

Turn up the heat and bring the syrup to a simmer. Don't stir it – you'll see lots of bubbles, then it will start to turn a little darker in colour and smell more caramelly. Cook for around five to ten minutes until it reaches 150°C. If you don't have a thermometer, drop a little of the syrup into your bowl of cold water – it's ready when it makes a hard ball as it cools.

When it's hot enough, take the pan off the heat. Quickly add the bicarbonate of soda and whisk vigorously. You'll see the honeycomb puff up – quickly tip it into your lined tin, then set aside to cool and harden.

Leftc
Cake

These are more suggestions than recipes. We realise that 12 portions of cake might be a lot for a family to get through, so this chapter is full of ideas to use them up and get the most out of your bakes.

Some of them – like the Caramel Brownie Sundae – are from our street food menu and make delicious puddings. Other ideas, like the Filled Savoury Scone and Toasted Cake, are great ways of using cake that might be about to go stale. Recipes like Cake Truffles and Leftover Cake Tiffin were born out of hating waste but have become so popular in the bakery we now have to bake cake specially for them. In some cases, like the Brioche Bread & Butter Pudding and Sticky Bun French Toast, it's worth doubling the recipe just so you can make these. And it might seem crazy to include something as simple as heating up cake, but our Hot Mess (hot cake with ice cream and our chocolate sauce) is a huge seller and it would feel all sorts of wrong not to mention it here.

We want leftover cake to become something you look forward to having in your house!

ver

Last Day Cake

Sometimes, after a day or two, cake is just not at its best, so here are some ideas to give it a new lease of life.

· These ideas work on bakes that are on their last day, but they won't fix stale cakes past their best.

· Don't be tempted to warm anything iced with buttercream. It just doesn't work and you'll end up with a curdled mess.

TOASTED CAKE

This works really well with things like muffins and undecorated loaves and cakes. Just heat a dry frying pan on a medium heat, and then toast slices of your leftover cake on both sides until it's gone golden and a little crispy. The Giant Lemon Drizzle (page 85), Breakfast Smoothie Muffin (page 23) or First Class Muffin (page 27) both make an amazing breakfast sliced into fat discs, toasted and served with Greek yoghurt and some Berry Compote (page 251).

HOT MESS

This is a huge hit on our street food menu. It's just cake, warmed through (in a microwave, preferably) and served with ice cream, Dark Chocolate Glaze (page 246) and Brown Sugar Glaze (page 248). We make it with any of the following: Caramel Brownie, Double Chocolate Muffins, Raspberry & White Chocolate Cookie Bars, Salted Caramel Crumble Bar and sometimes even one of the millionaires (making the messiest of all the Hot Messes). It may not be pretty but it is, we promise, delicious.

FILLED SAVOURY SCONES

It's not all sweet stuff. Filled Savoury Scones often make an appearance on our Sunday brunch menu and they go down a storm. Warm a cheese scone (page 51) through in a hot oven, then fill it with cooked bacon, scrambled eggs and a dollop of Spicy Tomato Sauce (page 307). It's also lovely with cooked, sliced vegetarian sausages and a softly poached egg.

Sticky Bun French Toast

This is a lovely way to use up leftover sticky buns and make a quick but indulgent special occasion sort of breakfast. It makes a soft French toast with a crunchy top, a little like bread and butter pudding, and is really good served with Berry Compote (page 251) or drizzled with maple syrup.

SERVES 1

1 medium egg
50ml full-fat milk
50ml cream (double or single)
1 tbsp sugar
¼ tsp vanilla extract
pinch of cinnamon (optional)
1 sticky bun
knob of butter

Whisk the egg, milk, cream, sugar, vanilla and cinnamon in a wide, shallow bowl. Cut the sticky bun in half horizontally and pop both pieces cut side down in the eggs for a minute or so. The cut side will soak up lots of the eggy cream. Briefly turn the buns over.

Heat the butter in a frying pan on medium heat. Fry the bun, cut side down, for two to three minutes or until golden brown and set. Turn the heat to low, turn the buns over and fry for another couple of minutes.

Brioche Bread & Butter Pudding

This may be in the leftover cake section, but to be honest we've been known to bake extra Raspberry Doughnut Brioche Buns (page 43) just so we can make this pudding. It's rich and comforting: a mix of puddingy soft bits and crispy edges dotted with the jam from the buns and fresh raspberries.

SERVES 6–8

35 x 24cm traybake tin, lined

8 medium eggs
400ml full-fat milk
240ml cream (double or single)
200g caster sugar
2 tsp vanilla extract
pinch of cinnamon (optional)
6 Raspberry Doughnut Brioche
   Buns (page 43)
150g punnet of fresh raspberries
3 tbsp light brown sugar
dusting of icing sugar to finish
   (optional)

Preheat the oven to 200°C (180°C fan).

Whisk the eggs, milk, cream, caster sugar, vanilla and cinnamon together. Cut each brioche into three vertically and line them up in rows in the pan: you want the slices to overlap a little so the surface isn't too flat. Sprinkle over the raspberries, tucking some between the layers of brioche.

Pour the egg mixture over the slices, then sprinkle with the light brown sugar. Bake on the middle shelf of the oven for 35 to 40 minutes until the egg mixture is set and the top is golden brown. Lightly dust with icing sugar before serving.

Variation

LEMON & BLUEBERRY BREAD & BUTTER PUDDING
Replace the brioche buns with six Lemon Drizzle Brioche Buns (page 44) and use blueberries instead of raspberries.

Cake Truffles

We started off making Cake Truffles to use up extra cake, but they are so popular now, we bake cake especially for them. They are so simple to make and look so cute! You can use any sort of leftover sponge and can fill and coat them with flavour combinations that complement the cake. It's worth freezing any small amounts of leftover buttercream and leftover sponge (particularly the trimmings from layer cakes) so you're never far away from making some. This basic recipe is based on six un-iced cupcakes, but you really can make them with any amount of cake. It's a very forgiving recipe.

- Make these with either cake leftovers that are within their use by date or freshly defrosted cake.

- It's hard to be exact as the amounts depend on how much cake you have, but if you need to make buttercream for six cupcakes you'll need about 150g soft, unsalted butter and 210g icing sugar. See instructions on page 233.

- If you'd like to fill your truffles, why not try a fresh raspberry, or a teaspoon of hazelnut spread, jam or caramel (chill the blobs on a piece of greaseproof first so they are easier to handle). Place the filling on a half truffle, then form a ball around it. Chill and coat as usual.

- These are best eaten on the day but can keep for another day in the fridge if your cake and buttercream are still within their use by date.

MAKES 6 LARGE TRUFFLES (OR 12 SMALL ONES)

6 un-iced cupcakes
8–10 tbsp buttercream (page 233)
300g chocolate, melted

Break up the cakes with your fingers until you have a bowl of crumbs with no big lumps. Stir in enough buttercream that the mixture holds together easily when you squeeze it together (don't make it too wet as that makes the truffles difficult to handle). Form into balls, then place on a lined tray in the fridge until they are solid and firm to the touch.

Melt the chocolate in a small, deep bowl and dip in each of the truffles so they're fully coated. Pop them back on a tray in the fridge till the chocolate has set. For a neater finish, trim away any set pooled chocolate from the bottom of the truffle.

Caramel Brownie Sundae

This is a big, gooey treat of a pudding and a perfect way to use up leftover brownies. It's a huge seller on our street food menu and, to be honest, it's worth making a batch of brownies and freezing some so you're never far away from making it. As with everything in this chapter, the amounts below are a suggestion and you can use as much or as little of the sauces as you fancy. We use both the Brown Sugar Glaze on page 248 and the Dark Chocolate Glaze on page 246 but you can always use shop-bought caramel and drizzle over some melted chocolate.

MAKES 2 SUNDAES

2 sundae glasses or small, deep
  bowls

1 slice Caramel Brownie (page 246)
½ batch Brown Sugar Glaze
  (page 248) or shop-bought
  caramel, warmed
½ batch Dark Chocolate Glaze
  (page 246) or melted chocolate
  to drizzle
4 small scoops vanilla ice cream

Warm the brownie for 30 seconds or so in the microwave, or wrap it in foil and put it in the oven at 180°C (160°C fan) for five to ten minutes. Then chop it up into big chunks. Place a big spoonful of both the brown sugar and chocolate glazes in the bottom of each bowl, followed by some brownie chunks, then a scoop of ice cream. Repeat the layers, then drizzle more chocolate glaze (or melted chocolate) all over.

Bad G
Savou

When we first opened, savoury wasn't a big part of our menu, but all that changed in 2020 when I realised we had to approach the savoury menu the same way we did the cakes: making sure all the recipes were indulgent, generous and most definitely a treat.

I can't take credit for most of the recipes in this chapter. That goes to Darren Campbell, our head chef, who took our vision and came up with a savoury menu to be proud of.

Here you'll find his burgers and bakes, all packed with flavour and texture. If he had a signature bake, it would be his sausage rolls. They are a firm favourite and sell out every day – when we first put them on the menu we wiped the local butcher out of sausage meat!

If you've never tackled puff pastry before, do have a look at his Rough Puff Pastry recipe on page 277. While there's no hiding the fact that it takes a long time to make, the actual hands-on part of the recipe is very straight forward, and nothing makes you feel more like a baker than making your own pastry. That said, all these recipes will work a treat with shop-bought pastry, so feel free to use that if you don't have the time or inclination to make your own.

Girl
ry

Rough Puff Pastry

Darren has been making puff pastry for 15 years and he swears by this recipe. It makes lovely, flaky, buttery pastry. Anyone who's ever made puff pastry from scratch knows that it's a long, time-consuming process. Rough Puff Pastry is a much quicker version that gives great results.

There is absolutely nothing wrong with good shop-bought pastry, so do feel free to use that, but if you fancy making your own pastry for the sausage rolls and savoury pastries in this chapter, then give this a go. The method might, on first reading, look very complicated, but if you break it down it is just a series of rolling out and folding the dough. If you think of it like that and do it stage by stage, you'll see how simple it is.

We have also made a vegan version (page 280) with a few tweaks.

- Make sure the butter and water are very cold. If you're making the vegan version, don't use vegan spread – make sure you use plant-based butter.

- Omit the seasoning for sweet puff pastry.

- Resting the dough is important, so don't skip the chilling-in-the-fridge steps.

- Once you've made the pastry dough, it can be chilled overnight and used the next morning, but bear in mind it will be harder to roll out when it's fridge cold.

- This recipe makes enough for eight turnovers (page 299), six sausage rolls (page 283) or six breakfast bakes (page 302). The quantities can easily be halved.

cont.

rolling pin
ruler or tape measure

240g unsalted butter, fridge cold
350g plain flour
120ml ice cold water
1 tsp vinegar (we use white wine
    vinegar, but any will do)
salt and pepper (for savoury
    pastry only)

As your hands get a little messy making this, it's a good idea to measure out all your ingredients before you start.

First, grate the butter and weigh out 40g and two lots of 100g. Pop the two 100g batches into separate bowls and put them back in the fridge. Weigh the flour into a mixing bowl and measure the ice water into a jug and add the vinegar.

Add a good pinch of salt and pepper (if you're making savoury pastry) to the flour and give it a mix with your fingers to combine. Take the first 40g of grated butter and rub it in with your fingers (as if you're making crumble) until it looks like breadcrumbs. You can do this part in a food processor if you like.

Make a well in the middle. Gradually add the ice water and vinegar mix, using your fingers in a claw shape to mix. Keep adding the water until the dough starts to come together – you may need to add a tablespoon or two more of water. Bring it together into a rough ball. Smooth out the ball of dough in your hands, wrap in cling film and pop it in the fridge for ten minutes.

Lightly flour your surface and roll out the pastry into an oblong shape about 40cm long and 20 to 25cm wide (it doesn't have to be exact), with the short edge closest to you. Take one of the bowls of grated butter out of the fridge and scatter it evenly all over the pastry.

Fold the bottom third of the pastry over, then fold the top third over that so you have a small fat packet with no butter showing. Roll it out into a large 40 x 25cm oblong, and then repeat the folds. Wrap in cling film and pop it in the fridge for ten minutes.

Roll the pastry out again to 40 x 25cm. Take the final 100g butter out of the fridge and scatter it evenly over the pastry. Fold the bottom and top edges over as before, then roll it out and repeat the folds. Rewrap and pop the dough back in the fridge for another ten minutes.

Roll the pastry out into the large oblong – this time we don't cover it in butter – and fold the bottom and top edges over. Roll out one final time, repeat the folds, then wrap and chill in the fridge for an hour.

It's now ready to use.

Vegan Rough Puff Pastry

V

We wanted to create the same buttery, flaky pastry for our vegan customers and I was absolutely delighted with the first version I tested, so here it is. You'd be hard pushed to tell the difference between this and the butter version.

The vegan pastry needs a bit more help to create the richness of the buttery version, so it has a little more fat and seasoning.

250g unsalted plant-based butter, frozen for at least two hours
350g plain flour
1 tsp salt (for savoury pastry only)
150ml ice cold water
2 tsp vinegar (we use white wine vinegar, but any will do)
pepper (for savoury pastry only)

Follow the method on pages 277-278, with the following tweaks:

· Weigh the grated frozen butter into 50g and two lots of 100g.

· Go easy when you're adding the water – you may not need it all.

280 · · · · · · · BAD GIRL BAKERY | Bad Girl Savoury

Shortcrust Pastry

Shortcrust is surprisingly easy to make. This recipe is the one Darren was taught to make at the start of his career and we use it for all the savoury quiches and pies in this chapter. For vegan shortcrust, use plant-based butter (not soft spread) – you may need a little more water.

- Make sure the butter and water are very cold.

- Take time to smooth out the cracks in the pastry before you put it in the fridge to rest.

- Resting it is important, so don't skip it.

- Once you've made the pastry, it can be chilled overnight and used the next morning, but bear in mind it will be harder to roll out when it's fridge cold.

- Add just enough water to bring the dough together. Too much water will make the pastry hard.

MAKES ENOUGH FOR A LARGE 25CM QUICHE (OR 4 PIES USING USING A 10CM PIE TIN)

400g plain flour
200g unsalted butter or plant-based butter, fridge cold
100ml ice cold water
salt and pepper

As your hands get a little messy making this, it's a good idea to measure out all your ingredients before you start.

Weigh out the flour into a big mixing bowl and add a generous pinch of salt and pepper. Chop the butter into small cubes and measure the ice water into a jug.

Give the flour, salt and pepper a mix with your fingers to combine. Add the butter and rub it in with your fingers (as if you're making crumble) until it looks like breadcrumbs. You can do this part in a food processor if you like.

Make a well in the middle. Add the ice water a third at a time and, using your fingers in a claw shape, mix until the dough starts to come together in a rough ball. You might not need all the water, but if you're making vegan shortcrust, you may need a tablespoon or so more.

In your hands, smooth any cracks out in the ball of dough, then wrap the dough in cling film and pop it in the fridge for at least 30 minutes. It's now ready to use.

Bad Girl Sausage Rolls

Of all the savoury bakes we make, this one is the favourite by far. Our head chef, Darren, is a demon sausage roll maker, and this is his recipe. We scaled it down (just a little) to make it easier to make at home. As always it's absolutely fine to use shop-bought puff pastry.

- Do try it with the horseradish and mustard, even if you're not a fan. They intensify the savoury flavours and act as seasoning more than flavouring.

- Wet your hands before rolling the filling into sausages as this prevents it from sticking to your hands.

- These are best served warm out of the oven, but once cooled they can be stored in the fridge for up to three days.

- If you're not eating them straight away, it's best to cool them quickly and get them in the fridge as soon as possible. Reheat at 180°C (160°C fan) for about 20 to 25 minutes until the centre is piping hot.

MAKES 6

large baking tray, lined

900g pork sausage meat
    (we recommend getting
    it from the butcher)
1 heaped tsp horseradish sauce
1 heaped tsp wholegrain mustard
¼ tsp pepper
1 batch of Rough Puff Pastry
    (page 277) or 375g ready-rolled
    shop-bought puff pastry
1 egg
splash of milk

Preheat the oven to 210°C (190°C fan).

In a big bowl, mix the sausage meat, horseradish, mustard and pepper. Split the seasoned sausage meat into six 150g balls.

Roll the pastry out on a lightly floured surface. If you've made your own, cut the block into two pieces and roll each one into a rectangle roughly 39 x 18cm (if your edges are ragged, roll it a bit bigger so you can trim it to the right size. If you're using ready-rolled shop-bought pastry, cut the rectangle in half and roll each one to the sizes above. Cut each pastry rectangle into three smaller rectangles.

cont.

Divide your filling into six equal portions. Lightly roll one into a long sausage shape (don't press too hard), making sure it's long enough to go slightly over each end of a pastry rectangle. Put the sausage a third of the way down on a piece of pastry and roll it up, tucking the edge of the pastry under as you go. Repeat with the other five. Once they are all rolled, you can cut them into halves or thirds to make party-sized sausage rolls, but adjust the baking times down a little.

Beat the egg with a splash of milk and brush it over the tops and sides of the sausage rolls. Place them on your lined baking tray and bake on the middle shelf of the oven for 30 to 35 minutes, until the filling is piping hot and the pastry is golden brown.

Allow to sit on baking tray for five minutes before serving.

Variation

VEGAN SAUSAGE ROLLS

Use the Vegan Rough Puff Pastry recipe on page 280, a vegan hard cheese and vegan sausages. The pastry can be glazed with soya milk instead of egg wash.

Bad Girl Pies

Pies are a mainstay of our savoury menu and the recipes below are firm favourites. We make them with the Shortcrust Pastry recipe on page 281 but feel free to use shop-bought instead if you fancy. We use 10cm individual pie tins that are 3cm deep.

- The fillings need to be cool before you put them in the pastry cases – we often make them the day before.

- Fill and bake the pies when you are ready to eat them, as we don't recommend reheating them.

- If you don't have individual pie moulds, you can make one big pie, but you'll need to blind bake the pastry base first. If you need them, details on how to do that are in our quiche recipe on page 296. You'll also need to adjust the baking time.

- You could also use the fillings to make savoury puff pastry bakes following the method on page 302.

SERVES 4

4 x 10cm pie tins (at least 3cm deep)

1 batch of Shortcrust Pastry (page 281) or 375g ready-rolled shop-bought shortcrust
1 batch of filling (page 296-301)
1 egg
splash of water or milk

Preheat the oven to 200°C (180°C fan).

Lightly flour your surface and roll out the pastry into a rectangle about 50 x 30cm. Cut four circles of pastry, each about 2cm larger than your pie tin. Re-roll the pastry and cut out four slightly smaller circles using the bottom of your pie tin as a template. You'll need to re-roll the scraps, but go easy on the flour when you re-roll as it can dry out the pastry.

Gently press the larger circles into the tins and up the sides. Divide your chosen filling between the pastry cases, then place a pastry lid over the top of each. Fold the excess pastry from the sides over, squeezing to seal as you go.

Brush the top of each pie with egg wash (or plant-based milk if you're making the vegan Spiced Roast Vegetable Pie). Put the pies on a baking tray on the middle shelf of your oven and bake for 40 to 45 minutes until the top is golden brown and the centre is piping hot. Serve immediately.

Spiced Roast Vegetable Pie

V

These pies are jam-packed with roast vegetables and full of wonderful textures, colours and flavour. We spice the filling with our spice rub on page 307, but feel free to use Cajun seasoning or a pinch of chilli flakes instead, or try stirring a spoonful or two of vegan pesto through just before you fill the pies.

The pies will look very full, but don't worry – the filling will settle. Brush the top of the pies with either soya milk or some melted plant-based butter (instead of the egg wash) before you bake them.

300g chestnut mushrooms, halved
500g butternut squash, cut into
   small chunks
2 small red onions, quartered
4 garlic cloves
1 tbsp Pulled Pork Rub (page 307)
4 tbsp olive oil
200g cherry tomatoes
salt and pepper

Preheat the oven to 200°C (180°C fan).

Spread the mushrooms, butternut squash, onions and garlic on the baking sheet and sprinkle over the rub, a bit of salt and pepper and the olive oil. Mix with your hands until all the veg are well coated. Roast for 20 minutes, stirring halfway through, then add the whole cherry tomatoes and roast for another ten minutes. Check that all the veg are tender and roast a bit longer if not. Set aside to cool, then discard the garlic cloves. Assemble and bake the pies following the instructions on page 289.

Braised Beef & Ale Pie

This is perfect winter comfort food, the kind of thing you might make on a rainy Sunday. The recipe started life as Darren's Braised Beef Pie, which was amazing as it was, but I was keen to incorporate an ale from our friends at Black Isle Brewery, so we tweaked it and added their Porter and this recipe was born. It's packed with meat (there's no veg to bulk it out) and it is rich, hearty and filling.

1 tbsp vegetable oil

1kg stewing steak (with a little fat)

1 small onion, roughly chopped

3 garlic cloves, crushed

1 vegetable stock cube

300ml ale (we use Black Isle Brewery Porter but any dark ale will work)

1 tbsp tomato purée

4 tbsp instant gravy granules

1 tbsp brown sauce

1 tbsp light brown sugar

salt and pepper

Put the kettle on to boil. Heat the oil in a big saucepan over a medium heat, then fry off the beef until it's browned all over. Add the onion and garlic and gently fry for a couple of minutes until soft.

Dissolve the stock in a litre of boiling water and add this, the ale and the tomato purée to the pan and bring everything to the boil.

Turn the heat down a little and let it simmer vigorously for two to three hours, stirring every so often. Keep an eye on the liquid levels and top up with more boiling water if it looks a little dry – Darren usually ends up adding about three litres in total as it cooks down a lot. When the meat is soft and falling apart, stir in the gravy granules, brown sauce and sugar, and cook for another five minutes. Taste to see if it needs salt and pepper.

Decant the filling into a large dish in a cool place. As soon as it's cool enough, pop it in the fridge to cool completely. Assemble and bake the pies following the instructions on page 289.

Chip Shop Chicken Curry Pie

This recipe is from our lovely friend, chef Sean Toye. Sean worked with us for a little while and introduced these mild curry pies to our menu. If you love a chip shop curry sauce, this is the pie for you: it's really easy to make and the filling is lovely on its own too.

3 skinless chicken breasts
   chopped into 1–2cm chunks
1½ tbsp mild curry powder
1 small white onion, roughly
   chopped
4 garlic cloves, crushed
1 tbsp olive oil
1 tsp ground cumin
½ tsp turmeric
pinch of chilli flakes (optional)
½ vegetable stock cube
1 tsp salt
1 tbsp cornflour

Sprinkle the chicken with half a teaspoon of the curry powder and set it aside to marinate a little.

In a large frying pan over a medium heat, fry the onions and garlic in the olive oil until soft. Add the chicken and fry, stirring all the time, for two or three minutes before adding in the rest of the curry powder and the cumin, turmeric and chilli flakes. Continue to fry until the chicken is cooked (about 10 minutes), then add 400ml boiling water and crumble in the stock cube and salt. Bring to a boil, then turn the heat down to a low simmer for 10 to 15 minutes.

Mix the cornflour with a little water and stir it into the chicken, then simmer gently until the sauce thickens. Check for seasoning and adjust to taste.

Decant the chicken into a large dish in a cool place (if the filling is in a shallow layer it will cool quickly). As soon as it's cool enough, pop it in the fridge to cool completely. Assemble and bake the pies following the instructions on page 289.

Pulled Pork Pie

We are all huge fans of pulled pork, but until recently we only used it in our Pulled Pork Loaded Fries (page 304). Then one day we had some left over and tried it in a pie, and it's been a favourite ever since. Whether you want to make a pie or not, this recipe is a great one to have up your sleeve anyway: it's so easy. Although it takes a long time in the oven, the hands-on part of the recipe takes no time at all. The pork needs to be cool before you fill the pies, so you can always make it the day before if that's easier; the flavours are even deeper the next day.

1kg pork shoulder
1 tbsp olive oil
5 tsp Pulled Pork Rub (page 307)
1 red onion, roughly chopped
3 garlic cloves, crushed
330ml Coca-Cola (not diet)
4–5 tbsp Spicy Tomato Sauce
    (page 307) or shop-bought
    BBQ sauce
100g mature Cheddar, grated
    (optional)

Put the kettle on to boil and preheat the oven to 190°C (170°C fan).

Cut the skin off your pork shoulder (leaving on the fat) and rub the olive oil all over it, then the spice rub. Put it in a large roasting tin and scatter round the onion and garlic, then pour in the Coke and a litre of boiling water. Place in the oven for four to six hours, until the pork is falling apart and tender.

Lift the pork out of the roasting tin and into a big bowl, and pull it to shreds with two forks. Stir through the Spicy Tomato Sauce and three to four tablespoons of the juices from the tin – you want it nice and juicy. Decant the pulled pork into a large dish in a cool place (if the filling is in a shallow layer it will cool quickly), and as soon as it's cool enough, pop it in the fridge to cool completely. Assemble and bake the pies following the instructions on page 289. If you're using the Cheddar, put about 25g on top of the pulled pork in each pie before you put on the pastry lid.

Mushroom, Spinach & Parmesan Quiche

We call this jam-packed quiche because it's so generously filled and full of flavour. It is a big seller, especially in the summer, but we often play around with fillings, so feel free to change things up. We've put a few suggestions below.

- If you don't have baking beans, you can use dried pasta, rice or dried peas.

- Adjust the seasoning according to the fillings you are using. We don't use a lot of salt as the Parmesan is quite salty. You might need even less if you use something like salty bacon.

- Make sure you put your quiche in the oven on a baking tray. It stops the pastry overhang baking onto the shelves and stops any leaks messing up your oven.

- If you're not eating this warm, cover and put in the fridge as soon as it's cool and eat within three days.

SERVES 6–8

25cm fluted tart tin, at least 4cm high, greased with butter on bottom and sides
baking beans (see Handy Hints if you don't have any)

1 batch of Shortcrust Pastry (page 281) or 375g ready-rolled shortcrust pastry
2 tbsp olive oil
500g chestnut mushrooms, cleaned and quartered
125g spinach
100g Parmesan cheese, grated

Preheat the oven to 200°C (180°C fan).

Lightly flour your surface and roll out the pastry into a circle about 5–6cm larger than your tin all round (you might need to roll out shop-bought pastry a little more to make it big enough). Roll the pastry onto your rolling pin and place it over the tin, then use your fingers to lightly press it into the tin. You should have excess pastry hanging over the edge. Rip off a little of the pastry overhang and roll it into a ball, then use this to press the pastry firmly into the sides of the tin (without having to worry about piercing it with your fingernails). Prick the base all over with a fork.

cont.

6 medium eggs
100ml double cream
200ml milk
½ tsp salt
¼ tsp ground black pepper
½ tsp wholegrain mustard
    (optional)

Line the pastry case with a circle of parchment big enough to cover the sides too and half-fill with baking beans (or rice or whatever you are using). Place on a baking tray and bake for 20 to 25 minutes, then take it out and remove the baking beans and paper and bake for another 10 to 15 minutes or until the pastry is light golden brown.

While the pastry case is cooking, heat the oil in a pan and fry the mushrooms on high until they start to colour and give off a little water. Add the spinach and cook until it is wilted and any moisture has cooked off. Set aside to cool.

Take the pastry case out of the oven and immediately sprinkle half the Parmesan evenly over the base so it melts. This helps to prevent your filling leaking out of any cracks.

Drain and discard any juices from the mushrooms and spinach, then spread them over the Parmesan. Whisk the eggs, cream, milk, salt, pepper and mustard (if using) together, then add the rest of the Parmesan. Pour it into the pastry case: it will look very full but it will all fit.

Bake on the middle shelf of the oven for 30 minutes or until the top is golden brown and the surface set. You should feel a very slight wobble in the centre. If it's not quite done, pop it back in for five minutes and check again. Allow to cool on the tray for five minutes or so before you trim off the excess pastry with a sharp knife. It's ready to serve.

Variations
Using the same quantities of egg, milk and cream, you can change the fillings – just make sure whatever you use fills the case around half full. We like:

cooked lardons, chunks of Brie and dollops of cranberry sauce

cherry tomatoes and grated mozzarella (which is lovely if you whisk a heaped tablespoon of green or red pesto into the egg mixture)

Mozzarella, Pesto & Cherry Tomato Turnovers

This is a lovely bake to make for lunch. It's incredibly easy to make (even easier if you're using shop-bought pastry), takes minutes to assemble and looks really beautiful. You can of course vary the fillings to suit your tastes, and because you're basically assembling ingredients you can make turnovers with different fillings in the same batch.

- For this recipe you want the harder mozzarella that comes in a block – sometimes labelled mozzarella for pizza – rather than the softer balls.

- To make vegan turnovers, use the Vegan Rough Puff Pastry recipe on page 280, a vegan hard cheese and vegan pesto. The pastry can be glazed with soya milk.

- These are best served warm out of the oven, but once cooled they can be stored in the fridge for up to three days.

MAKES 4

large baking tray, lined

12 cherry tomatoes, quartered
4 heaped tbsp basil pesto
200g mozzarella
½ batch of Rough Puff Pastry
   (page 277) or 375g ready-rolled
   shop-bought puff pastry
1 egg
splash of milk

Preheat the oven to 210°C (190°C fan).

Put the tomatoes in a small bowl and mix with the pesto. Slice the mozzarella into four rectangles.

Lightly flour your surface and roll out the pastry into a square about 28cm across. Don't worry if your edges are raggedy; they will be trimmed off. If you're using shop-bought pastry, you might not need to roll it out much. Trim to a 26cm square, then cut it into quarters to give you four evenly sized 13cm squares.

cont.

Divide the tomato and pesto mixture into four and arrange diagonally over the centre of each square, but don't spread it to the edges of the pastry: there should be about 2cm of pastry showing at either corner (this means the filling won't ooze out too much when you bake it). Place a rectangle of mozzarella over the top of the pesto, again keeping a margin of pastry at either corner.

Make an egg wash by beating the egg with a splash of milk, then dab a little on one of the corners of pastry opposite the long edge of the filling. Fold the opposite corner over the filling, then fold the egg washed corner over (the egg wash is the glue that holds the pastry together) and press the join down with a fork.

Brush the tops of the pastries with egg wash and place them on your lined baking tray. Bake on the middle shelf of your oven for 25 minutes, or until the pastry is cooked through and golden brown and the cheese has melted.

Allow to sit on the baking tray for five minutes before serving.

Variations
You can vary the fillings endlessly: this is a great way of using up leftovers, especially odd ends of cheese. We like:

a tablespoon of cranberry sauce and a slab of Brie

a slice of cooked bacon and a slab of Cheddar

a few slices of ready-to-eat chorizo and a slab of smoked Cheddar

Loaded Fries

V

This isn't really a recipe, more a good idea for combining whatever you have kicking about in the kitchen. In the café, we always braise big batches of beef and make huge amounts of pulled pork so we can make pies, sliders and these.

Our Loaded Fries are piled high with toppings, then baked until they are a gooey, melty mountain, perfect for a weekend treat. Our favourite combinations are below, but you can easily mix things up. We use skinny fries, but you could try chunky chips, sweet potato wedges or even nachos. The amounts are entirely up to you – make them as generous or restrained as you fancy.

SERVES 2 AS A SIDE, 1 AS A MAIN

For Pulled Pork Loaded Fries and Smoked Cheddar Fries:
500g cooked, hot fries
large spoonful of hot Pulled Pork
    (page 295)
drizzle of Spicy Tomato Sauce
    (page 307) or shop-bought BBQ
    sauce
100g smoked Cheddar cheese,
    grated

For Braised Beef, Onion & Cheddar Fries:
500g cooked, hot fries
large spoonful of hot Braised Beef
    & Ale (page 291)
dollop of onion chutney (optional)
100g mature Cheddar cheese,
    grated

Get the oven on at 200°C (180°C fan).

Pile up the fries in a small heatproof dish (we often use small enamel pie dishes), then dollop as much meat as you fancy on top. Drizzle over the sauce or chutney, then top with grated cheese and bake for five to ten minutes until the cheese is melted and oozing.

GF V

Spicy Tomato Sauce

This is tangy and sweet and has a bit of a kick. We use it in our Pulled Pork on page 295, in the Filled Savoury Scones on page 263 and in our Sunday Breakfast Bakes on page 302. It's also great in toasties and on burgers too.

· This will keep in a sterilised jar in the fridge for up to a week. If you like more of a kick, add more chilli.

MAKES 350ML

1 tbsp oil
1 small onion, finely chopped
5 garlic cloves, crushed
1 tbsp tomato purée
90g dark brown sugar
2 tsp smoked paprika
1 tsp garlic powder
¼ tsp crushed chilli flakes
3 tbsp white wine vinegar
400g tin chopped tomatoes
salt and pepper

Get the oven on at 200°C (180°C fan). Heat a tablespoon of oil in your saucepan over a low heat and fry the onion and garlic gently until the onion is soft. Add the tomato purée and cook for another five minutes. Stir in the sugar and cook for another few minutes until the sugar has melted. Finally, add the smoked paprika, garlic powder, chilli flakes and vinegar, give it a mix and add the chopped tomatoes. Bring to a boil, then simmer on a low heat for 20 minutes, stirring frequently – it can catch and burn so don't leave it. It will thicken up while you cook it. Taste for seasoning and then blitz with a stick blender till smooth or mash with a potato masher.

GF V

Pulled Pork Rub

This is the rub we use in our Pulled Pork (page 295) and in the vegan Spiced Roast Vegetable Pie (page 290).

· If you like more of a kick, add more chilli to taste.

· This will keep its flavour in a clean, dry jar for up to three months if the spices are relatively fresh.

2 tsp smoked paprika
1 tsp garlic powder
1 tsp crushed chilli flakes
4 tbsp dark brown sugar
2 tsp crushed black pepper
1 tsp ground cumin
1 tsp rosemary
1 tsp sea salt flakes
1 tsp Cajun seasoning (optional)

Just mix everything up and decant it into a clean, bone-dry jar.

Brioche Burger Buns

These are so satisfying to make! They are light, fluffy and not at all sweet but for all their lightness they are robust enough to hold up to Bad Girl-sized burgers and sliders really well. They make excellent sandwiches, and are also lovely filled with ice cream and our Brown Sugar Glaze (page 248). Huge thanks to Graeme Ayton of Scottish Bakers for all his brioche advice.

- We always make brioche dough in a stand mixer as it's hard work making it by hand, but if you want to try it see the notes at the end.

- Start the dough the day before you want to make the buns: it needs to be refrigerated overnight.

- These are best the day they're made but are still fine the day after.

- Make sure you keep an eye on your mixer while it's running. Ours nearly fell off the table after vibrating very close to the edge!

MAKES 6

large baking tray, lined and lightly oiled

200g strong white bread flour
50g plain flour
25g caster sugar
1 tsp salt
7g sachet fast action yeast
60ml milk, slightly warmed
3 medium eggs
125g unsalted butter, softened and cubed
1 egg, beaten

Weigh out the bread flour and plain flour, sugar and salt into the bowl of your stand mixer and give them a stir to combine. Add the yeast, milk and eggs and mix at low speed for 10 to 15 minutes. You'll have to scrape down the bowl and paddle a couple of times.

By now your dough should be smooth-looking and stretchy – give it a wee pull to check. Keep the mixer on low and add two or three cubes of butter at a time. You can't rush this stage, I'm afraid, so don't add any more butter until you can't see any trace of the last lot.

Once the butter has all been added, keep mixing until the dough has come away from the sides of the mixer. Scrape the dough out and put in a well-oiled bowl, cover with cling film and pop in the fridge overnight.

cont.

Bad Girl Beef Burger

This is the first burger we put on our hot food menu and it remains a firm favourite with our customers, served with candied bacon, strong Cheddar and bacon mayo. The bacon fat is one of the things that makes it so very tasty, so don't be put off by it. Use the fatty part of bacon rashers and save the medallions to serve with the burger. It will come as no surprise that these are big burgers, with two patties in each bun.

- It's best not to season the raw burger mixture as it can make the burgers tough. Season the raw patties just before you fry them.

- Make sure you toast the buns. Not only does It add flavour, but it helps to stop them getting soggy and falling apart.

- To check if the burgers are cooked through, cut into the thickest part of the burger. No one will see once the burger is built!

- To candy bacon, sprinkle a little brown sugar over it and cook in the oven to your liking. Turn it over halfway through and sprinkle the other side with sugar as well.

SERVES 2

2 tbsp oil
1 small onion, finely chopped
2 cloves of garlic, crushed
500g beef mince (20% fat is best)
50–100g bacon fat, diced (as much as you can get from one packet of bacon)
½ tsp horseradish sauce
½ tsp wholegrain mustard
1 medium egg
salt and cracked black pepper

Get the oven on at 200°C (180°C fan) and pop a baking tray in to preheat.

Heat a tablespoon of oil in a big frying pan over a low heat, then gently fry the onion and garlic until the onion is soft.

Put the mince, diced bacon fat, horseradish, mustard and egg in a big bowl and mix together. Add the slightly cooled fried onion and stir till combined.

You can, at this stage, divide the mix into two and make one thick burger per person, but we like to divide it into four. Not only do the thinner patties take less time to cook, but by putting two in each bun you can layer the fillings, making the finished burgers really tall and impressive. Season the patties on both sides.

cont.

To finish:
strong Cheddar, sliced
2 Brioche Burger Buns (page 309),
    halved
3 tbsp mayo
1 tomato, sliced
iceberg lettuce
streaky bacon, cooked

Wipe out your frying pan and heat another tablespoon of oil on a high heat. Fry the burgers on both sides for a couple of minutes until golden brown, then transfer them to the hot baking tray and put in the oven for eight to ten minutes until cooked through. If you've made thicker burgers, you'll need to cook them longer.

If you like your cheese melted on the burger, put a slice on top of the burgers when they're nearly cooked and pop back in the oven for a minute or so until the cheese melts.

Wipe the frying pan clean and put it back over a medium heat. Toast the brioche bun halves cut side down in the dry pan.

Spread mayo on both halves of the buns, then layer from the bottom up in the following order to keep the burger as crispy as possible: tomato, lettuce, the first patty, a piece of streaky bacon, the second patty, then the cheese.

Crispy Chicken Burger

We serve these lightly spiced, crispy-coated chicken breasts in a brioche roll with iceberg lettuce, tomato and pesto mayo. It's really quick and simple but tastes great!

- Get organised before you start. Coating the chicken is a messy business and your hands will get covered, so you don't want to be rummaging round the kitchen at this point.

- Don't skip toasting the buns. Not only does it add flavour but it helps to stop the buns getting soggy and falling apart.

- If you don't like pesto, try flavouring the mayo with a few drops of sriracha or sweet chilli sauce instead.

- To make breadcrumbs, take three slices of bread, lay them flat on a baking tray and put them in the oven at 170°C (150°C fan) for 20 minutes or so, until the bread is dried through and toasted. Whizz in the processor to make crumbs.

SERVES 2

baking tray, lightly oiled

100g plain flour
1 tbsp smoked paprika
2 eggs
100ml milk
100g breadcrumbs
1 large chicken breast
1–2 tbsp oil for frying
salt and pepper

To finish:
2 Brioche Burger Buns (page 309)
3 tbsp mayonnaise
2 tsp basil pesto
1 tomato, sliced
iceberg lettuce

Preheat the oven to 200°C (180°C fan).

Put the flour in a wide shallow bowl with the paprika and a good pinch of salt and pepper. Beat the eggs into the milk in another bowl and put the breadcrumbs in a third.

Butterfly the chicken breast – that is, cut it horizontally through the middle so you end up with two thinner pieces. Dip the chicken in the flour so it's well coated, then dip it in the egg, then repeat (doing this twice means the coating will be really crispy). Finally, coat the chicken pieces really well in the breadcrumbs, pressing down gently to make sure they stick.

Heat a tablespoon of oil in a big frying pan over a medium heat. Fry the chicken breasts till golden brown on the bottom, then turn and fry the other side – approximately two to three minutes per side. You may need to add another tablespoon of oil when you turn the chicken over.

cont.

Pop the chicken pieces on a lightly oiled baking tray and bake in the centre of the oven for five to ten minutes. Check they're done by cutting into the thickest part – the time will vary depending on the thickness of the chicken pieces, so don't go by time alone.

While the chicken is finishing off in the oven, clean the frying pan and put it back over a medium heat. Toast the brioche buns, cut side down, in the dry pan so the inside gets nice and browned.

Mix the mayo and pesto, then spread most of it on the bottom half of each bun. Then add a couple of slices of tomato and then the lettuce (this order keeps the burger as crispy as possible). Slice each piece of crispy chicken horizontally in two and stack them on the lettuce to create height, then top with the bun lid spread with the rest of the pesto mayo.

Falafel Burger

Whether you're a vegetarian or not, do give these a try. They're quick and easy to make from store cupboard ingredients, but they taste fantastic and make a perfect weekend lunch. We shape the mix into burgers, but you can also roll into balls and either serve them in a tomato sauce, or in pitta bread with hummus and salad. Add a pinch of chilli flakes to the chickpeas if you like a bit of a kick.

- Don't skip toasting the buns. Not only does it add flavour but it helps to stop the buns getting soggy and falling apart.

- If you don't like pesto, try flavouring the mayo with a few drops of sriracha or sweet chilli sauce instead.

- To make this gluten-free, use gluten-free bread for the breadcrumbs.

SERVES 2

1 slice brown bread
2 tbsp oil
1 small onion, finely chopped
2 cloves garlic, crushed
400g tin chickpeas, drained and
  rinsed
1 tsp ground cumin
1 tsp turmeric
1 medium egg
salt and pepper

To finish:
2 Brioche Burger Buns (page 309)
3 tbsp mayonnaise
2 tsp basil pesto
1 tomato, sliced
iceberg lettuce

Get the oven on at 170°C (150°C fan).

First make the breadcrumbs. Dry out the bread in the oven for 20 minutes or so, and when it's cool crumble it up, or grate it to make breadcrumbs.

Turn the oven up to 200°C (180°C fan).

Next, heat a tablespoon of oil in a big frying pan over a low heat and fry the onion and garlic gently until the onion is soft and transparent. Turn the heat up to medium and add the chickpeas, cumin and turmeric. Fry until everything looks dry, and set aside to cool.

Once the mixture is cool season with salt and pepper, then put it in a wide jug or bowl. Add the breadcrumbs and the egg and blitz with a stick blender. You can also mash with a fork instead, which will give you a chunkier texture. Divide the mix into two and form into burger shapes – the thickness is up to you, but we like ours thick!

cont.

Wipe out your frying pan, then put in a tablespoon of oil and put over a high heat. Fry the falafel burgers on both sides for a couple of minutes until golden brown, then transfer to the oven for five to seven minutes until cooked through.

While the falafel is finishing off in the oven, wipe the oil out of the frying pan and put it back over a medium heat. Toast the brioche buns, cut side down, in the dry pan so the inside gets nice and browned.

Mix the mayo and pesto together, then spread most of it on the bottom half of the buns. Layer on the tomato slices, then the lettuce, then the burger (this order keeps the burger as crispy as possible). Spread the rest of the pesto mayo on the bun lids and put them on top.